TAKING OFF

the

Mask of Secrecy

FINDING THE LIGHT AFTER
THIRTY YEARS OF DARKNESS

PATTY LAUTERJUNG

Published by Victorious You Press™
Charlotte NC, USA

TITLE: TAKING OFF THE MASK OF SECRECY
First Printed: 2023

Cover Designer: Nadia Monsano
Editor: Lynn Braxton

ISBN: 978-1-952756-99-3

Printed in the United States of America

For details email joan@victoriousyoupress.com
or visit us at www.victoriousyoupress.com

DEDICATION

To Mother and Dad, who encouraged me with their words and led by example, to have a strong work ethic, learn through reading and education, and make excellence a priority. Mother's words are a constant source of motivation, "Patricia, you can do anything you put your mind to."

To my son Paul, you inspire me with your strength of character, godly wisdom, and devotion to your family. You help me move forward in life and make being your mother God's greatest gift to me.

To my granddaughters, Addison and Isabella, who make my life as a grandmother truly meaningful and memorable. I leave a legacy to you through my writing.

Most importantly, to my Lord and Savior, Jesus Christ. You've surrounded me with interesting people, challenging experiences, and new opportunities in order to do the creative and fulfilling work You planned for me. May I honor You by being obedient to my purpose in life to serve others, build relationships, and leave a Christian legacy.

close friendships. Our time together as roommates and leaders in the Marin Covenant Church youth staff is priceless and will always bring fond memories.

To Lynn Braxton, Joan T. Randall, and Nadia Monsano—As my editor, publisher, and website designer, I am in awe that God answered my specific prayers when I moved here and brought you to me. Each of you has helped me fulfill the purpose He has for my life. Lynn, your incredible editing has made my story come alive and brought out the best in me. The laughter we shared as creative editors, and the tears we cried, as I revealed my tender wounds, have created a priceless friendship.

Thank you all for making me a better version of who God created me to be.

TABLE OF CONTENTS

FOREWORD

As a psychologist, I am fascinated with us humans. I have been studying us my entire adult life. I have counseled thousands over the years and had the distinct honor to be trusted with the stories and accounts of people's greatest fears, joys, and sorrows.

Here's what I know for sure about what it means to be a human.

Not one human in the course of the history of time has ever completed their human life without experiencing some form of suffering.

Here's what I know about suffering.

The more we resist suffering, the longer it stays around.

The more we silence our suffering, the louder it becomes.

The more we label suffering as *bad* or *getting worse,* the more intense it gets.

The more we avoid our suffering, the more frequently it comes for a visit.

As a psychologist, I know that whatever we think we can't have or hold only gets bigger and heavier.

As a psychologist, I also know what gives suffering power and what takes its power away.

Secrets hate truth-tellers like Patty. When people like her share stories like this, the oxygen supply for shame is cut off.

When beautiful humans like Patty share their greatest suffering with others, something profound happens. We don't become immune from suffering, but the experience of shared suffering lightens the load...for all of us.

The humanity in me can meet the humanity in you.

A collective "Me too" is heard and experienced between us.

"Oh, you have suffered? Me too."

Let this book function as a map back home to yourself. The you that can show up for all that it means to be a human. Let Patty's story and lessons ignite hope and provide strategies for you to make meaning of your suffering. So that you can let go of it.

There can be great joy after great suffering.

My greatest prayer has always been, "God, don't let me waste my suffering."

Pain has been my growth accelerator. Let it be yours.

–Dr. Erin Oksol

INTRODUCTION

According to the National Domestic Violence Hotline (NDVH),[1] one in four women (24%) and one in seven men (14%) have experienced some form of physical violence by an intimate partner. Are you one of those frightful statistics? Chances are, if you're reading this, either you've experienced abuse or know of someone who has.

For almost thirty years, I allowed the abuse by my husband to continue because I never took the bold step to get the help I truly needed. There were a variety of reasons why I kept the abuse to myself, hidden behind a mask of secrecy. You will learn what caused my silence by reading this book, *Taking Off the Mask of Secrecy, Finding the Light After Thirty Years of Darkness*. You will also understand why I didn't recognize the abuse at first because it wasn't physical but was verbal, emotional, and financial. I don't want anyone to suffer as long as I did, and I specifically describe behavior like—reckless driving, sarcasm,

---

[1] NDVH, "Domestic Violence Statistics," November 2022
https://www.thehotline.org/stakeholders/domestic-violence-statistics/

minimizing actions, and being blamed for frequent unemployment—as examples of abuse. The opinions, experiences, and statistics expressed are written from my perspective and accurate to the best of my ability.

Abuse usually starts slowly and infrequently and builds over time. You will learn about the common trap of *trauma bonding* that keeps people in an abusive relationship. As you read and begin to identify with my story in some way, even if it's to help someone else, my hope is that you will take the first step of courage toward freedom.

The shame that I carried for years drove me into isolation. Pastor Steven Furtick of Elevation Church says, "If the shame runs deep, His grace runs deeper than you think." It wasn't until I got into a Christian recovery program that I started to let go of the shame, guilt, embarrassment, and fear that kept me in bondage.

Whether you believe in the power of God, the universe, nature, or whatever brings meaning to your life, there is wisdom in learning from my mistakes. Mine is also a story of victory, purpose, and freedom that comes when you take action to change. You may not feel it now, but let's get started together to reveal the unique, valuable, and significant person you are.

Part 1
HOW DID I GET HERE?

Have you ever asked yourself, "How did I get here? This wasn't what I thought would happen to me. I had my life planned differently. Why did this happen to me?"

We can ask ourselves this question when something unexpectedly great happens. I've had some amazing experiences, a few I consider miracles, that you will hear about. Perhaps a wonderful memory is flashing through your mind right now.

For most of us, it's the dramatic event we didn't see coming that makes us question ourselves. This section leads up to the most publicly humiliating and unexpected experience that changed my life forever.

If you or someone you know has been through a difficult situation, particularly abuse in its various forms, this section begins the journey towards recovery. It's not all doom and gloom. Hopefully, you will feel encouraged, engaged, and entertained by my story—one that many people can relate to.

AND THEY LIVED HAPPILY EVER AFTER

When you were young, what dreams did you have about your future? Mine were like most girls my age—marry Prince Charming, have a baby, own a dream home, and live *happily ever after*. Unlike many girls in my neighborhood, I had three brothers and spent my time building forts, playing football and baseball, and climbing trees. Being a tomboy was a great time in life because of the outdoor adventures, physical activity, and opportunities to use my imagination. This is probably where my passion for creativity began. However, my innocent thinking and choices eventually turned my dream into a nightmare.

Mike was a childhood friend I had known for two years. He was athletic, and we enjoyed playing team sports and hiking in the hills overlooking beautiful San Francisco and the Golden Gate Bridge. Our friendship got serious, and he wanted to marry me. Mike wrote me a romantic note with our initials inside a heart. I blushed and giggled when he gave it to me, followed by a kiss. I carried that treasure with me everywhere.

One day, we had a disagreement. It wasn't the first time we argued.

"Mike, I don't like how you talk mean to me and call me names. You aren't my Prince Charming." I took the note out of my pocket, tore it into pieces, and threw it on the ground.

Without warning, Mike punched me sharply in the stomach. "If you tell anyone, you stupid idiot, I'll hit you again," he scowled in anger.

With tears streaming down my face, I whispered, "I won't."

Just then, the school bell rang. All the kids from our third-grade class ran inside, including Mike. I wiped away the tears, took a few deep breaths, and tried to smile as I quickly walked into class and sat down. Mrs. Hutchinson was my favorite teacher, but I was afraid to tell her after Mike threatened me. I also didn't want to be a *tattle tale*. I kept my eyes down, still in shock at what happened and tried to get over the pain in my stomach.

Kids were laughing and talking while we waited for class to start. Mike sat in the row of desks next to me, and out of the corner of my eye, I saw him get up and walk towards me. I thought he might be coming over to say he was sorry. As I looked up, he glared at me, and I looked back down. He walked behind me towards the water fountain, and hit me hard in the back with his fist, and whispered, "Weirdo."

I gasped for air and put my head on my desk to hide the tears.

"Go tell the teacher!" my friend, Linda, demanded. I kept my head down, keeping silent.

As Mike walked back to his desk, I kept my head down, hoping he wouldn't bother me again. Then, excruciating pain radiated through my body as he punched me in my back again as hard as he could. Tears quickly filled my eyes.

"Crybaby," he teased.

This time, two students cried out, "Patricia, tell the teacher!"

Just as the bell rang, I lifted my head and saw Mrs. Hutchinson staring in my direction.

"Patricia, what's going on back there? I'm hearing your name being called by several kids. You're one of my best-behaved students."

I took a deep breath and wiped my eyes. The classroom was quiet.

"Tell her," Linda said.

I slowly stood up, looked at her, and said softly, "Mike has been hitting me."

Mrs. Hutchinson and all the other students looked at him, but I kept my eyes straight ahead.

"Michael and Patricia, I want to talk to you outside in the hallway."

My heart was pounding as I walked past everyone, feeling embarrassed that they were all staring at me, including my closest friend, Linda. Outside, I felt safe with Mrs. Hutchinson nearby. Mike and I told her our sides of the story.

"Patricia, you should have come to me and not kept this a secret," she calmly explained. I nodded my head in agreement.

"Michael, hitting others, especially girls, is wrong. I don't ever want you to hit another student again," she said sternly. "I will not tolerate name-calling. You need to say you're sorry for your hurtful behavior."

Mike shuffled his feet, looked down, and in a monotone voice said, "I'm sorry."

"I forgive you," I softly responded as I stared at him. There was no expression on his face. Our friendship was over, and he never spoke to me or hit me again.

Without realizing it, that experience with Mike of childish infatuation, emotional reactions, tolerance of verbal and physical abuse, and fear of public embarrassment, began an unhealthy pattern of behavior and choices that would continue into my adulthood.

God would use this defining moment to eventually, in His timing, release the hurt child within me. My story is the result of God's faithfulness and plan to take my childhood dream and create a meaningful life for me. But the bigger story is not *about* me but what He can do *through* me to help others. That perspective gives me the freedom to be vulnerable about many details of my life because God is the author of what I write.

LAYING THE FOUNDATION OF CREATIVITY

My parents believed in a well-rounded education, and my creativity flourished in fourth grade when I studied the violin. I dreamed of being a violinist in the San Francisco Symphony across the bay from where I lived in Tiburon, California. I practiced seven days a week for the entire school year. I still have the practice chart to prove it! My music teacher played trumpet with the Symphony. One day, he wrote on my chart, "Pat is very talented for music and a hard worker, which gives her the combination to become an excellent violinist!"

In eighth grade, I was invited to join the Redwood High School Honor Orchestra and quickly learned, as a twelve-year-old, the need to <u>earn</u> the respect of seventeen and eighteen-year-olds. I admired the poise and talent of the first violinist, and I worked hard that school year to perfect my playing as a member of this prestigious group of musicians.

When I graduated, I found out I would be attending a Catholic high school that did not have an orchestra. Despite my talent and interest in the violin, there was no plan by my parents to continue because of the expense of private lessons. What I didn't know, was that God had other plans to develop my creativity in music.

That summer I went to Girl Scout camp. The camp counselor played the guitar, and I became fascinated with it. "Diane, would you teach me how to play?" I asked.

Without hesitating, she said, "Sure, Pat! Sit down by the fire, and let me show you how."

Within a week, Diane taught me a few chords and how to strum. I wrote down her songs that included "Michael Rowed the Boat Ashore," "If I Had a Hammer," and the famous camp song "Kumbaya." My older brother, Pete, had a guitar, and when I got home from camp, he let me borrow it. I taught myself to play sitting in front of a weekly TV show called, "Play Guitar with Laura Webber." Remarkably, I forgot about my dream as a concert violinist—it no longer seemed possible in my young mind—and devoted my time to the guitar. I was happy to create music again.

I'm not a therapist but have received enough help from them to know that my past, consciously and sub-consciously, has impacted me. The answer to "How did I get here?" in my abusive marriage, likely began with my mindset in the honor orchestra. I was out of my comfort zone, seeking acceptance and attention, and I was willing to sacrifice time and maintain strict discipline to reach a dream I thought would make me happy. This experience motivated me to strive for what I thought was excellence. My well-respected music teacher believed I would be an "excellent violinist," and so did I.

I didn't realize so young that *excellence* and *perfection* are not the same. What started out as an opportunity to use my interest and talent for something I enjoyed turned into dysfunctional behavior to be perfect. As I got into high school and college, I began to develop migraine headaches from the pressure I put on myself to be perfect. I thought they were inherited from my mother who suffered from them for years any time something—or someone—upset her. Migraines and frequent headaches plagued me for years until I understood the emotional and physical reasons for mine and made choices and changes that ended them.

My mother often told me, "Patricia, whatever you put your mind to, you can do." Mother loved to read and learn, and my passion for books and writing is her legacy. Her eyes lit up when she talked about flowers and plants, and Mother's beautiful garden was a source of visual joy filled with fragrant aromas for everyone. Mother used to say, "My garden is my therapy." I understood that as I got older and became aware of her way of dealing with the problems of life was to pray and work in her garden. I may not have inherited my mother's "green thumb," but working in a yard, walking through a nursery, and nurturing my plants reminds me of her and warms my heart.

I admired my dad for his work ethic and numerous awards as a decorated military officer. Dad had high standards and expectations, and I developed the belief that hard work equaled success and respect. When I came home with all A's except one B in Math, my dad frowned at me, crossed his arms, and said in a harsh voice, "What's the matter with you? Weren't you paying attention?" There were no encouraging words about my other grades. Reliving this memory brings tears to my eyes. I learned years later when Dad and I grew close, that he had an authoritarian father and emotionally distant mother, and he realized he was repeating what he had learned. There were sad memories Dad had never talked about, even with my mother. Over time I saw him soften as his faith in God got stronger, and he was able to share about the pain he had carried inside for years.

Both of my parents were smart—in fact, the school wanted my mother to skip a grade, but her mother said no—and I loved to learn from a very young age. My IQ was tested at 120 (superior intelligence) in the top 9 percent of the population. I don't say that to impress you but to let you know there were expectations on me, either real or imagined, to succeed.

I wanted to please my parents, and I began to put high expectations of achievement on myself in school and activities like sports and music. I was elected president of my school, editor of the school newspaper, excelled in team sports, and was consistently on the honor roll.

The desire to make my parents proud of me with my music, impress them with my leadership roles, and bring home excellent report cards and awards in sports had me focused on the outside of who I wanted to be. Subsequently, I spent a lot of time alone in my room and found it hard to develop any close relationships outside of the one with my brother Richard. There were girls my age in the neighborhood, but I was shy and felt more comfortable around rowdy, adventurous boys.

"Patricia, why don't you go play with Linda?" my mother would ask to encourage me to play with the other girl on my street.

I always had an excuse like, "I have to practice my violin," or "There's a spelling test tomorrow I need to study for," or "Linda likes to play with dolls. I just want to twist their heads off." I'm NOT making that last comment up! My mother wrote in my baby book, "Patricia likes to play with guns and twist the heads off her dolls." I'm sure there is a deep, psychological explanation for my aggressive behavior as a child, but I assure you...I've outgrown it...I think!

My drive for what I thought of as success led to a twenty-year-old *perfectionist overachiever*. I don't particularly care for labels because I think it creates a certain image and limitations on people. I only use this to give you an idea of the behavior that would be carried into my relationships.

I received my Associate of Arts degree in Liberal Arts from a local college, got my first job at a local bakery, tutored college students, and quickly started saving money. While there were serious discussions with my brothers about careers, I wanted to be a teacher. My parents said, "Patricia, if you want to attend a university, you will have to pay for it yourself." I was determined to succeed and enrolled at the University of San Francisco. My parents were rightly skeptical of my decision, and after one semester between tuition, books, and other expenses, I was back at the local college working on another degree.

IS HE THE ONE FOR ME?

I never forgot about my dream to marry Prince Charming. I thought about it through high school and college. Looking back, I may have been academically intelligent, but my relationship standards at twenty-one years old were very low—smart, good looking, a job, and fun to be with. I have no idea where my values ranked...but qualities like integrity, commitment, family, and faith apparently were not on my radar. That was a recipe for disaster!

I dated a good-looking guy named Dennis in college. He had all the *superficial* qualities I was looking for. My heart raced whenever I looked into his deep blue eyes, and dreamily watched as he stroked his surfer-blond hair as we held hands in his convertible sports car. We were both young and immature, and in less than a year were engaged. I was raised a strict Catholic, and Dennis joined the Catholic religion so he could marry me in the Catholic Church. We had a big church wedding in beautiful Tiburon. At twenty-two, I thought I had found Prince Charming.

My dream was coming true, and it included an opportunity to use my creativity in music. I worked as the secretary at St. Hilary's Catholic School, led a group of singers and musicians at church, and loved teaching guitar lessons after school. Two of my students were Malik and Faun Pointer, children of the famous singers The Pointer Sisters. I was invited to dinner at their grandmother's home in Sausalito and was in awe of the Platinum Record Awards hanging on the wall. Years later, I felt humbled when Malik contacted me through social media to thank me for teaching him to play guitar. He had started a band. I told him, "You were a handful of trouble in grammar school, but I'm so proud of you for what you've done with your life and your band." I still keep in touch. You never know the positive impact you can make in other people's lives, despite problems in your own life.

Dennis worked for a while in sales for Bruce Sedley, the inventor of the "zoo key" for the storybooks at the San Francisco Zoo and the magnetic card key that we all use today to unlock doors. Bruce was also a ventriloquist and host of many San Francisco Bay Area children's TV programs. Dennis helped him with personal appearances as "Skipper Sedley" and his beloved puppet "King Fuddle" of Fairyland in Oakland, California. I was thankful Dennis had a job so we could save a little money for the future. This was the "fun" time in our marriage that I wanted, but it would soon end.

Dennis came home from work one day with a frown on his face and slumped down in a chair. "I'm tired and depressed being a salesman and dressing up in silly costumes for children. I'm going to apply to the city academy to become a policeman."

"Oh, sweetheart. That's such a dangerous job, but I want you to be happy," I said as nervous tension filled my body. "I'll support whatever you decide to do."

Dennis was smart, took classes while he worked part time, and was quickly hired. The values I should have waited for in a husband became wedges that separated us. He told me, "I don't want to have children," and I cried and felt devastated. I started on birth control pills and didn't tell my parents because I felt ashamed I wouldn't have children and didn't think they would understand. My Catholic faith kept me praying for a miracle, but I felt empty inside and didn't feel I could talk to anyone about it.

I was committed to my marriage for life. But my heart ached when Dennis said, "I don't want to go to church anymore. I work late and want to sleep in the morning." As a new wife, I didn't want us to argue. Neither Dennis nor I had learned from our parents how to handle conflict. So, we didn't discuss it any further, and I kept my feelings and emotions to myself.

I continued to go to church by myself, too embarrassed to tell my family and afraid they would be angry at Dennis. After a few months, I stopped attending because I wanted us to be physically close on Sunday mornings. I also daydreamed about being a mother and prayed he would change his mind about having children.

Dennis was never physically or verbally abusive, but over time he emotionally withdrew from me. I often cried and lost sleep worrying about his safety as he confidently walked out the door in his crisp and polished police uniform. We spent less time enjoying life together as his ambition to advance in the police department took priority with late-night work, self-development classes, and overtime. Our intimacy as a young married couple diminished, and with no plans to have children, I was losing interest in sex with him. To compensate for my feelings of loneliness, I kept myself busy at work, obsessively cleaned the house, and spent hours playing my guitar.

After three and a half years of marriage, Dennis shocked me one day when he announced, "I want a separation to get my life together." It never occurred to me that we might ever divorce.

My parents had been married for thirty years, and even with problems, divorce was not an option. Dad used to joke, "I would never divorce your mother. I couldn't financially afford it!"

But it was no joke that my childhood dream to marry Prince Charming, have a baby, own a nice home, and live happily ever after began to look like a nightmare!

I was so naïve at twenty-five and believed we would soon reunite. I was willing to do whatever he wanted and give him most of our material possessions. When I told Mother through tears, "I'm packing a few items today for my apartment and leaving the rest for Dennis," she drove over to the house where we were living with Dennis' mother and grandmother. They weren't home, and Mother began putting our lamps, small furniture, and anything else she could fit in her station wagon. I tried to stop her insisting, "I don't need that now. We'll be back together soon." Mother ignored me and kept packing. I didn't understand then, as I do now, that it's not selfish to take care of yourself.

Within a few weeks, Dennis called, and said, "I moved out of Mom's house and am living with a police buddy. I've had time to think, and I want a divorce."

"But we've only been apart a few weeks. I still love you," I pleaded.

"You're not changing my mind," he firmly declared.

"I'm going to Lake Tahoe tomorrow with my parents. Maybe we can talk when I get back," I sighed, my hands shaking as I slowly hung up the phone.

Mom and Dad picked me up the next morning, and as we turned the corner down my street, my heart skipped a beat when I saw a familiar car parked in front of the apartment building. "There's Dennis' car. That's where his police friend must live who he just moved in with."

Without hesitation, my mother said, "He's not living with a guy. I'll bet you money that he's shacking up with a woman!" Dad was silent.

"I don't believe that, Mom!" I insisted. "That's his friend's apartment." We didn't say much more about it, but I started to feel betrayed and lied to. I decided to enjoy the weekend in Tahoe as much as I could and check it out when I got back.

Two days later, Dennis' car was still there and Mom said, "Mark my words. He's living with a woman."

My heart broke, but I held back the tears. I unpacked my suitcase, and then went to sit in my car where I could see the apartment building. I knew Dennis would be leaving for work soon. Sure enough, a door opened, and he walked down to his car and drove away. My hands were shaking as I walked up the stairs to find the apartment number. I went to the group mailboxes and found the number and name "Kathy S" on it. My heart was pounding, and I had a hard time breathing from the shock of this discovery. I went home, and in the phonebook found the name at that address. My eyes began to water as I thought about Mother's words, "He's living with a woman." I wiped away the tears and thought, *There's a way I can quickly find out.*

I called my mom and said, "In three minutes, call this number. I can't tell you why right now, but if anyone answers, hang up." She agreed, and I anxiously ran down the street and up the stairs.

I carefully peered in the apartment window draped with lace curtains. I saw our clock and a few more familiar items. Suddenly, I was startled when the phone rang inside the apartment. I didn't wait to see who answered...I didn't want to know what she looked like. My hands were shaking and my legs felt unsteady as I grabbed the hand rail and quickly walked down the stairs and back to my apartment.

Mom comforted me as I told her what she already knew. With a calm and reassuring voice, she said, "We'll get a divorce lawyer." I got off the phone and cried and cried. My dream to find Prince Charming had turned into a nightmare.

I drove to the police department and confronted Dennis in the parking lot. He was surprised to see me. I was angry and glared at him. "I know about you and Kathy," I said through gritted teeth. "I'll give you the divorce!"

His response was cold. "Good. Just don't come here again." No apologies for his deception and lying. Nothing.

Because there was credit card debt and a loan to supplement our income, the divorce settlement left me almost financially broke. It was not the last time I would deal with credit card debt and loans in a relationship. The next time would be the most traumatic nightmare of my life. I asked myself, "How did I get here?"

IT'S MY PARENTS' FAULT!

"I didn't break that vase. Richard did!!" "My husband can't find a job. He told our son, 'It's because your mother never encourages me. It's not easy to find work at my age.'" Have you ever blamed <u>someone else</u> for something that was really your fault? Have <u>you</u> ever been accused of anything that was not your responsibility? If you're like most people, the answer is yes to both questions. Each situation gives us an opportunity to control the only thing we can, and that is our mindset and the response that follows. It's interesting to think about our words and actions as they relate to abuse and the question, "How did I get here?" It involves responsibility.

I was a shy child, followed rules wherever I was, and was known for being "helpful and well-behaved." For me, blaming others happened as my reaction usually to fear of consequences knowing I had been disobedient and done something wrong. Sometimes it was hard to remember my side of the story to prove my innocence when I had to explain to Mother what my younger brother Richard had apparently done instead of me.

I thought Mother must have had "eyes in the back of her head." She knew my behavior well enough to recognize biting my nails and talking fast as a sign I was lying. With a frown on her face, she would usually send me to my room saying, "Go there and close the door. Think about what you've done. When you're ready to tell the truth, you can come out."

Sometimes, I would reflect on what really happened and pray, "Dear Jesus, help me to act better." Other times, I would play or read. It was important to please my mother because seeing her smile made me feel happy. I also wanted to go outside to play, so I usually walked out in a few minutes hanging my head and my shoulders drooping. After I confessed the truth, Mother would smile, hug me, and say, "Go outside and play." That was the end of my consequences.

When Mother's gentle and persistent voice couldn't stop Richard and me from arguing, we heard the dreaded words, "Just wait until your father gets home." This immediately stopped us, and we often cried and begged her to change her mind, but she would be silent. I habitually looked for ways to clean the house and be helpful. Richard would often go to the backyard to find more spiders to collect or take care of the honey bees he was raising.

Being on our best behavior usually resulted in us hearing, "Okay, I won't tell your father." You could hear a sigh of relief from us. When mother didn't change her mind, and Dad got home, I would often run and hide in the back of my closet. I trembled in fear until he found me, yelled criticism like, "You can't do anything right," and spank me with a ruler or belt. I learned to be a people pleaser and keep secrets from my dad.

I was never taught by my parents through words or actions how to handle conflict in a healthy way. When I was wrongly accused, I became defensive and usually angry. Rarely did my brother and I take individual responsibility, and we frequently both got punished by being spanked with a ruler or belt. When Richard and I were alone, we sometimes argued about who was wrong and resolved it by a wrestling match, teasing each other, or name calling until one of us gave in.

I didn't hold a grudge against Richard once the conflict was over. We are two years apart, and the fact we shared a room until I was twelve probably contributed to a "let's get along" attitude. Richard might have a different perspective on my stories. Whatever his memory is, we are still close, and he has always had my back for as long as I can remember.

For years I blamed my parents for who I had become after my divorce from Dennis. The role of *victim* was easy to fall into because I didn't want to take responsibility for my part in the breakup of the relationship. Blaming others got me nowhere, stuck in my dysfunctional behavior. Instead of saying, "You're the reason for this," a healthier response could have been, "I feel betrayed, hurt, and don't trust anyone right now. I'm going to get support to understand and learn from this experience, rely on God's help to do it, and take action to change the issues and habits in my life that contributed to the marriage problems. I need to focus on becoming a mentally, emotionally, physically, and spiritually strong person."

Yet, I carried the victim's attitude for years, thinking I couldn't do anything about what happened in my life. But unless we are children, who often truly <u>are</u> victims, the truth is there is always something we could have done. It may not have prevented the unexpected punch in the face or kick to our back, but the action we take that follows is certainly within our control, even if it can't be done immediately. The issue of thinking we are *victims* is a critical factor in abuse.

Over the years, I've found that one healthy change leads to another. It's harder, more time consuming, and sometimes close to impossible, to go back and fix something that is shattered and broken instead of <u>doing it right the first time</u>. I know from years of experience, research, and talking to thousands of people, that we can only change ourselves.

I believe it's important that instead of thinking of ourselves as victims, we change our perspective to *survivors*. A survivor says, "Yes, something awful and abusive happened, but I'm going to take care of it." The first time I was physically abused, I didn't know how to be a survivor, and this led to future incidents and a mask of secrecy that I wore for years. The purpose in sharing my story is that you, or someone you know, will become a thriving survivor, no matter where you are now in your journey. By picking up this book, you are taking the first steps towards freedom from abuse and a better life. I promise that it's possible!

After my divorce, choosing a victim role led to excuses not to change. The most destructive, hurtful, and crippling justification was, "I'm an adult child of an alcoholic father and emotionally distant mother. I was never taught what healthy behavior looks like, how to set boundaries, or good ways to handle conflict. I can't help the way I am. This is how I was raised." Just writing this brings a flood of tears from the hurt, anger, and disrespect I showed my parents.

I'm showing this personal vulnerability to let you know that blaming them was the worst choice I could have made when I was young because it opened the door to years of dysfunctional behavior, bad choices, allowing abuse to continue, and a mask of secrecy that imprisoned me. Words cannot truly express how thankful I am to God that I changed later in life and developed an incredibly close and meaningful relationship with both my father and mother.

I wrote individual tributes to my parents for Mother's Day and Father's Day to express my love for them and the impact they had on my life. I wrote them a year apart because it took me longer to personally work through the issues I had with my dad and reach the point where the words were from my heart. When I read each one out loud, tears filled our eyes, especially for my normally reserved dad. He and I connected on a deep level that day, and it led to the close relationship I had longed for as his daughter. I had the tributes framed, and Mom and Dad put them up in their home. I tearfully took them down when my brother, Peter, and I sold their home after Mom passed away. Here is some of what I said to each of them.

I thank God for you, Mother. You have been a wonderful example of what it means to love unconditionally and to teach me the importance of having God in my life.

I treasure the time we spend together. We both look forward to meeting for lunch every Thursday and plan our schedules around this time. You always buy me lunch and share the bacon from your BLT with Paul Jr. You also bring him a box of animal cookies. One time you forgot, and he cried. You have never forgotten since.

I get my youthful looks from you, Mother. Part of it is hereditary, but you have often said, "Life is too short to worry about things." You have such a positive attitude after seventy-seven years of life, even though circumstances could have given you good reason to be negative. This is the quality I admire most in you!

You believe in me. This, next to your strong faith in God, has made a big difference in my life. When others have doubted my abilities, you have been the one to say, "If you just put your mind to it, I know you can do it." Many of my successes in life are due to those words of encouragement.

Mother, you are a gift from God to me, and I will always love you. Happy Mother's Day.

Your daughter, Patricia

A TRIBUTE TO MY DAD

Today is a very significant day in my life. It is the beginning of a new relationship I have with you, Dad. There is no other daughter in the world who has more honor, love, and respect for her father than I have for you today. I feel like you and I have struggled together through good times and bad to reach this point in our lives. The Bible says trials build character, and I thank God you have been there to help me through many of them.

People have often said I am reliable. They can count on me to get something done and do it well. I think doing things excellently is your greatest strength and shows in whatever your hand touches.

I have learned to love and accept you for who you are. It was not easy for me to do at certain times in my life. The love of my Heavenly Father has helped me to cherish you, Dad. You are a gift from God to me, and I will always love you. Happy Father's Day.

Your daughter, Patricia

My parents are both gone, but I still feel their presence around me. We have a choice regarding the legacy we leave in this world. Mine is changing from victim to survivor. What will yours be?

Taking Off the Mask of Secrecy | 37

REBELLION AND REDEMPTION

At twenty-six I was now alone, ashamed of being divorced, tired of trying to be perfect, and ready to rebel against the meaningless life I had created. My safety net was I had a good job at an insurance company, was a hard worker and quick learner, and I was young. For the next four years, I turned my back on God. I didn't spend too much time with my parents and brothers, and I only told them about my achievements and never about my fears or sinful behavior. My mask of secrecy went with me everywhere, and I became an expert at hiding the truth about my life and past.

I joined social groups at work, went to parties, started drinking, became sexually promiscuous, built a network of influential people throughout the company, and secretly dated single executives. Note, I said <u>single</u>. Despite occasional advances in the past by married men, I quickly cut them off short, clearly stated my boundaries, and have <u>never</u> allowed myself to overstep them. It's sadly interesting that when it came to abuse in marriage, the same assertiveness and strict boundaries didn't exist.

With feelings of shame, hurt, and mistrust, I didn't allow people to get too close to me emotionally, and then I met a woman named Marilyn. We worked in the same department and surprisingly to me, quickly became friends. She was divorced with two young children, and I enjoyed spending time with her family when I wasn't socializing at parties and carrying on my loose lifestyle.

One afternoon, Marilyn said, "Would you like to come to my church's Singles Group? We're meeting this Monday at my house."

I said, "The roof will fall in if I walk through the door. I don't really belong in a church group with stuffy, boring church ladies." As soon as I said that, Marilyn's eyes opened wide, she got a big smile on her face, and we started laughing. She was anything but stuffy or boring, so I said, "Yes."

That group is where I developed new friendships, and found I wasn't alone in divorce. I never felt judged for my lifestyle by Marilyn or anyone in the group, and people openly shared private details about their lives that I wasn't used to hearing. It seemed like everyone had problems, but the difference was they talked about their personal relationship with Jesus that helped them through life. I didn't understand this different spiritual perspective and was quiet at first because I felt uncomfortable. I was raised Catholic, had a strong belief in God, and didn't relate to other religious beliefs outside of what I knew as the *one true church*.

When Marilyn invited me to her church, even though I had stopped going to the Catholic church for years, I thought hers might be a *cult,* and quickly said, "No." There was no evidence for me to believe Marin Covenant was a cult, and Marilyn didn't argue with me about my opinion.

She listened to me, answered my questions, and said, "Don't look at me as a Christian example to follow. I'm a terrible sinner. Jesus is the One you need to follow." I thought about what she said, and decided to attend church with her that Sunday. I was nervous and felt guilty when I walked in that I was doing something against my Catholic beliefs. I was surprised that I loved the worship music and the preaching was out of the Bible and meaningful to me.

I studied and learned over the next few weeks that being a Christian wasn't a religion to follow but a personal relationship with God. It was an acknowledgement that I was a sinner, that Jesus died for my sins so that I could have eternal life with Him, and that I accepted Jesus as my Lord and Savior. It didn't mean that I needed to be perfect—that was a huge relief to me as a dysfunctional perfectionist—but I would do my best to follow what God said in the Bible and not the sinful world around me.

I was afraid my life as a Christian would be boring until one afternoon, I realized how terrified I was of dying, not knowing for sure if I would go to Heaven or hell for unforgiven sins I had committed. So, one night at a singles meeting, I invited Jesus into my life.

Some of you may not believe in God the way I do, or even acknowledge there is any god. People have the freedom to choose to follow the universe, nature, Islam or Buddhism, any church, or whatever gives meaning to their life. I am not here to judge anyone but to tell my story and help others who have experienced abuse. My journey involved finding a personal relationship with Jesus. Yours will be a different journey, and my desire for you is that it leads to freedom from abuse and secrecy.

FINDING THE FOUNTAIN OF YOUTH

I had no idea that my spiritual decision to become a Christian would radically change my life and allow me to begin to take off the mask of secrecy I had been wearing since I was a teenager. It opened opportunities to experience what true friendships were, not the superficial ones I was used to attracting because of my hang-ups. At thirty-two years old, I was a young Christian who was excited to learn about the Bible and use my knowledge, passion for serving, and leadership skills to impact the lives of others. I was in a women's Bible study group teaching what I had already learned.

A young and vibrant guy called me one evening and said, "Hi Patty, this is Ray Johnston. I'm the new youth pastor at Marin Covenant. I heard from several people that you are one of the best young leaders around. I know you're already active in the church and would like to invite you to be part of my youth staff."

I thought to myself, *You had me at 'You are one of the best leaders around.'* For the next five years, I volunteered my free time to build into the lives of junior high, high school, and college students in the Marin Covenant Church Youth Group (MCC). I felt young and energetic living an exciting life. These were the best years of my life.

Under Pastor Ray Johnston's leadership and that of the youth staff, the MCC Youth Group became a positive influence in the schools, homes, and community of Marin County, California. Hundreds of teenagers had their lives changed through epic youth events like yearly trips to Mexico. We built homes to replace crumbling shacks, remodeled churches, hosted children's Bible camps, and developed relationships with people of another culture and with each other. MCC had outreach events like waterskiing and snow ski retreats to Lake Tahoe and surrounding areas. There were Christian concerts with young artists like Amy Grant and Michael W. Smith. We volunteered hundreds of hours in the community for a variety of work projects.

The attraction of MCC Youth was our weekly Wednesday night meetings with food, music, and fellowship and Ray, myself, and others teaching a relevant life message. The heart of the group was the relationship building and teaching in small groups during the week, divided up by gender and school, and led by staff members. This was my favorite part of being a youth leader, and many of the girls I spent time with have become lifelong, treasured friends.

While I was a youth leader, Marilyn got married, and I stayed in her house and rented out the rooms to women from church. With the number of single ladies living there, usually only moving out because they got married, we fondly named it "The Bachelorette Pad." The house became a place for many of the students and youth staff to hang out, listen to music, bake cookies and eat food, plan youth events, have girls sleep over, laugh a lot and sometimes cry, and talk for hours about anything. Parents knew the home was a safe place for their kids, and lives were changed from the atmosphere of acceptance, building relationships, and a focus on Christian values. One teenage girl said, "I don't drink at parties on Friday nights anymore. I come and have fun at your house."

I would be remiss if I didn't mention the fabulous roommates who were part of the youth staff and had a significant influence on my life. There are tears in my eyes, but a smile on my face, as I can see their faces, hear their voices, and remember the priceless experiences we had together in the Bachelorette Pad. They taught me how to have strong friendships. Not because any of us are relationship experts but because we know what it feels like and the time and commitment it takes. I love each of you and am grateful that God brought you into my life.

Numerous marriages...and some divorces...have come out of the MCC Youth Group. Forty years later, some students remained single, and others have their own children and even grandchildren now. We have our own Facebook group, and I continue to find out the incredible impact that is being made throughout the world.

SOMEDAY MY PRINCE WILL COME

I was thirty-four and still had not found my real Prince Charming. I had kissed a lot of frogs...and a few guys at work and church...and had one marriage proposal I turned down. My career was thriving, I was blessed with significant purpose as a youth leader, and I was working on a Bachelor of Arts Degree in Business Management. I told people, "Whoever I marry will need to make me happier than I am single. My life is great!"

During a women's retreat, I wrote in my Bible at the end of Proverbs 31—the ideal wife chapter—the qualities I wanted in a husband. I wanted God to know who I was looking for. I had matured emotionally and spiritually, my values were established, and my marriage standards were high.

- Committed Christian
- Encourager to me and others
- Share my interest in sports and be athletic
- Family oriented and loves children
- Sense of humor and fun to be with
- Honest communication
- Respected in his role at work and ambitious.

In the Fall of 1986, I sat in church mesmerized by the tenor voice of the soloist. I thought, *Who is that handsome guy with the magnificent voice?* My heart sank when I saw his ring as he sat down next to an attractive woman. I sighed and thought, *He's married and must be a guest here.* I forgot about him.

Two weeks later, I was sitting in the high school Sunday school class and thought, *I'm never going to meet someone in here to marry.* I walked upstairs and saw a sign over a door that read "Singles." I went inside and was stunned by who I saw in the class. I said to myself, *What in the world is a married man doing teaching a singles class?* As he spoke, I looked at his hand and noticed the wedding ring was gone. I had mistaken his school ring for a wedding ring!

After class, I confidently walked up to the front and introduced myself. "I'm Patty Bohan. If the singles group ever needs a place to meet, my house is available."

"Thank you, Patty. I'm Paul Lauterjung and will keep that in mind."

My heart was beating fast as I gazed up into his blue-green eyes. I suddenly realized I was staring at him and could feel my face turning red. I smiled and said, "See you later," and felt like I floated into the church service. It was hard for me to concentrate on anything but Paul for the next hour. I knew nothing about him except that he was a singer and part of the singles group, and I was immediately interested in dating him.

Looking back, my thoughts and actions about relationships were led more by my heart and need to find a man to fulfill me rather than a healthy mindset and strong relationship with God. I was still that little girl looking for the romantic love of my Prince Charming.

After the church service, I walked in a daze out to the parking lot. I was pleasantly surprised to see Paul standing at his car near mine. With a big smile on my face, I said hello, and we talked for a while. I was excited to find out we worked in buildings next to each other across the street and lived only five miles apart. He invited me to lunch that afternoon, and we started dating.

Paul enjoyed making me laugh, brought flowers, and sang love songs to me. We both loved being romantic, holding hands, and cuddling. I felt safe with him because he never tried to force himself sexually on me like other guys I had dated. We had just met, and with blind eyes, I began to believe God had answered my years of prayer.

I took a break from evening college courses and volunteer youth ministry to focus on our relationship. I got advice about healthy dating standards from people I respected, and my parents seemed to like Paul. My brother Richard told him, "If you hurt my sister, I'll come after you with my shotgun." I don't know if he meant it, but I think that put some fear into Paul for a while.

We attended a Christian singles retreat in Santa Cruz, where Paul told me about his past, and I shared mine. He assured me God had changed him, and I believed him. We were both imperfect people who were looking for someone to make us feel complete. The problem was that the issues we both carried were hidden beneath our own masks.

I wanted to get my bachelor's degree, so I started taking classes again. A month later, Paul surprised me with a marriage proposal, and I immediately said, "Yes!" His charm and appearance swept me off my feet. I was jumping up and down with happiness, and Paul had a big smile on his face. I couldn't wait to show everyone my engagement ring.

Sadly, I was blind to any red flags that warned me of problems in our relationship. My life felt out of control working full time, studying nights and weekends, planning a big wedding, and buying a townhouse where Paul would live before we got married. In less than six months after meeting each other, we were engaged and making numerous critical decisions. There were many sleepless nights, and my head throbbed in pain from migraines. I still hadn't learned how to resolve conflict in a healthy way, and Paul made a few decisions without asking me. His reason was, "I'm just trying to be helpful. You need to trust me. I've got everything under control." Ignoring this red flag would open the door leading to abuse and secrecy.

I wanted my husband to be the leader of our family, and it seemed that learning to trust his decisions was part of being a submissive wife. My heart was right, but I wasn't taking time to pray or learn what submission truly meant from a Biblical perspective. God was waiting for me to trust Him to lead and be in control of my life. It would take me years to learn that submission wasn't about control but mutual love and respect. The abuse I experienced over the next thirty years would stem from human control, but turning control over to God would set me free from the secrecy and prison I lived in.

I walked down the aisle in a beautiful white wedding dress. On our wedding night, Paul took my Bible, signed his name, the date, and wrote "That's me!" at the bottom of my

Proverbs 31 list. My childhood dream was finally coming true!

Part 2

WHY IS THIS HAPPENING?

"Why did you stay so long?" A few people have been very blunt with their opinions and said, "I would have NEVER put up with what you did. I would have called the police the first time he hit me." Even now, as I write this, I can see the frown on their face, the disgust in their eyes, and hear the harsh tone of their voice. I've gotten better at not taking comments personally and feeling bad about myself for my past decisions.

On the other side of this question, many people couldn't relate to being in an abusive relationship but had compassionate and sympathetic feelings for me. Some of them knew others were being abused and understood it was a common problem. Yet, there are other women like me, who were in an abusive relationship or are struggling with one now. It's these women who get tears in their eyes when confronted with trying to answer this painful question which makes them recall the bitter memories of their past.

It's the mother who hesitates to talk about what she and her children are experiencing day in and day out. It's also the victorious survivor who knows that every woman's reason for staying is different.

You will hear more of my story, perhaps learn new and eye-opening insights about types of abuse in relationships, and find some answers to why abuse is happening to you. There are common issues to deal with before abuse starts, how to overcome during it, and outcomes that are better when hard choices are made. This section may help you talk to friends or family members who experience abuse or maybe to the abuser. I am not a certified counselor, but I am a messenger of information and experience to help others.

I NEVER SAW IT COMING

The day we were married, Paul had written in my Bible at the bottom of my "husband" list, "That's me!"

The problem with what I listed was who I <u>wanted</u> Paul to be. They say *hindsight is 20/20* meaning, it is easier to see something clearer after it's happened rather than when we're in the midst of it. I can see now that whether or not Paul fit all these qualities, I allowed my mind to see him that way when we met and quickly got engaged in four months.

The expression *love is blind* applied to me. During our engagement, most of my time was spent going to school and studying while working full time. I hadn't known Paul even a year before we got married. I was so busy and deep in love that I either didn't see or minimized controlling behavior that I justified as him being the leader I wanted in our relationship.

They say opposites attract, and in our case, the differences didn't strengthen our relationship but caused more conflict through a lack of acceptance of our individuality. For example, Paul didn't share my interest in sports, but he worked out at the gym and liked to ride a bike—so I saw him as athletic. He didn't play any sports and didn't really care to watch them in person or on TV. There's absolutely nothing wrong with not having an interest in sports. However, for me who loved to play baseball, football, basketball, tennis, volleyball, and golf and watch the World Series, Super Bowl, Wimbledon, and The Masters—there wasn't a lot of conversation and sports activity for us to share.

I went from watching and playing individual and team sports at least once a week down to sometimes only once a month. This choice almost eliminated a major source of interest and fun in my life. It contributed to poorer health and significant weight gain. One decision cost me years of harmful consequences.

If we went to a sports party, Paul didn't get into the game with the guys. I became overly concerned about him having a good time and often subdued my excitement with the sports fans to be more attentive to him. I also became jealous when he spent more time talking with the women than the men, and my attitude of "go talk to the guys" didn't help strengthen our relationship. There were a few occasions we went hiking, which we both enjoyed, and it's a shame we didn't make more time to share it together. I learned too late in our marriage how to allow my husband to enjoy an event his way and to feel secure in myself.

I am responsible for my decision to marry too quickly because I didn't know Paul well enough at a deeper personal level, and therefore overlooked the red flags that came up. Most importantly, I had not worked through my own issues of mistrust, perfectionism, workaholism, and codependency that I carried into my marriage. My strengths of commitment, service, leadership, giving, administration, and a lifelong desire to learn and grow helped in our relationship, but my issues allowed that mask of secrecy to cover up the hurt inside.

Despite the differences between Paul and me that became more evident after we were married, my A-type success-driven personality was softened by his charming, romantic, and relaxed manner. During many years of our marriage, I often felt stressed from a self-imposed sense of perfection and achievement. Paul found a way that helped me relax and enjoy life more...vacations.

Paul loved to travel, and our honeymoon was ten days long, followed by a trip to San Diego a few months later. Shortly after I graduated college, he said, "I want us to celebrate your graduation and birthday with a trip to New

York! I've researched discounts on airfare, hotels, meals, and we can see a Broadway show."

"New York? I'm not much of a traveler. Can't we go to someplace closer? We also can't afford it because we're still paying down our debt."

After Paul's few more "good reasons" why we should go, I said yes. We put it on his credit card, and he did most of the planning. The time away seemed to draw us closer together with new experiences, exciting places to see, romantic dinners in New York, and less responsibility away from home.

When we returned home from our trip, I was overcome with joy thinking about the great time we had in New York. However, I didn't realize a deadly pattern was beginning to develop that would plague our entire thirty years of marriage—reliance on credit to pay for what we didn't have in cash. The stress of financial hardship, an unhealthy lack of self-control, and no outside accountability or help would damage my dream within our first year together.

Come back with me to a morning when I was still a newlywed, but now with a degree in business and a recent promotion. We had a low mortgage on a condominium and kept a written budget. We had paid off my $6,000 in credit card debt, but there was stress making monthly payments on Paul's $20,000 in credit card, loans, and school debt. I was thirty-eight, and my biological clock was ticking as I thought about my dream to have a baby.

We sat at the kitchen table finishing breakfast when Paul asked, "Where is my blue shirt? I want to wear it to work."

"I washed it last night and need to iron it."

"Go iron it now," he said sternly.

"I need to leave for work. I'll iron it when I get home. There is an ironed white shirt in the closet."

Paul stood up, glared down at me, and said, "I want my blue one! You need to be submissive to me!"

I stared at him, confused, and said, "Yes, but not right now."

Without warning, Paul punched the side of my face with his fist, knocking my glasses to the floor. For a few seconds, I couldn't see as throbbing pain radiated near my eye. My hands trembled as I wiped away the tears. "Why did you hit me?"

"I'm sorry. I didn't mean to," he said and knelt down to hug me.

"Get away from me!" I yelled and ran into the bathroom. "Oh, my God! My face is bleeding, and my eye is swelling!"

Later, Paul came downstairs wearing his white shirt. "I'm sorry. Please forgive me. That will never happen again."

I glared at him and then turned away. "I'm going to call my mother to talk about what happened."

"Do you think that's necessary? I said I was sorry."

"I need my mother."

He frowned and walked out the front door.

As I glanced at my reflection in the mirror, I felt ashamed. I called Mother. She comforted my pain with words of love. We decided not to tell Dad because of what he might do to Paul.

After hanging up from Mother, I called my manager. "Sherry, I won't be in today. I'm not feeling well." I started to cry.

"Patty, are you okay? What's wrong? You can tell me."

Sherry and I were the same age, and we worked well together. I felt I could trust her with my shameful experience. After I explained what happened, she said, "I am so sorry, and it must be hard. I will keep this confidential. Stay home until your eye heals."

I don't remember what was said when Paul came home from work. I'm sure there were flowers, promises to change and that it would never happen again, forgiveness on my part, and physical closeness again. I know we kept it a secret from everyone, and I don't think my mother and I discussed it after that. This incident began the first of many unexpected outbursts of anger over the years, along with verbal, emotional, and financial abuse.

There's a term called *trauma bonding*. It is a deep, emotional attachment created by a cycle of abuse, kindness, and intimacy. The *abusive* person has qualities that include being charming but emotionally unpredictable, thoughtful, and gives gifts and physical affection. They blame you for their behavior, apologize for the abuse, and don't keep their promises to change. The abuser tries to isolate you from others and even says you are their soulmate and are meant to be together.

The *abused* person has traits that include continued trust and belief the abuser will change, with more focus on special times together. They feel embarrassed and shameful for their situation, protect the abuser and relationship through secrets, and feel unable to leave for reasons like finances, children, and fear of safety.

I didn't realize until just last year that what I experienced was trauma bonding. I may have been told that in counseling, but I don't remember. I discovered the term when I was editing a book for a woman who experienced it with her abuser. With tears streaming down my face, I cried out, "Oh, Lord, that's one of the reasons I stayed so long."

I have talked to many women who stayed in an abusive relationship because they received something emotionally from it. It sounds crazy if you've never experienced it. Now that I understand how I was emotionally manipulated after being abused, my hindsight *is* 20/20, and I can help others as part of the purpose God has for me.

As the saying goes, *you don't know what you don't know,* so please don't feel ashamed or ignorant. If you want to learn more about trauma bonding, there's a lot of information on the Internet. Now that you <u>do</u> know something about it, I hope you will take the time to look at your relationship to see if it's happening to you or someone you know. If it is, then please take action to get some help.

ABUSE AND THE SOUND OF SILENCE

How was conflict handled in the environment you grew up in? If you had a different opinion than someone else, were you allowed to express it? Was it okay to show feelings like disappointment, impatience, sadness, or anger? If it wasn't acceptable to have a different opinion or show certain feelings, how did you deal with it?

When I was a teenager, the singing group Simon & Garfunkel had the #1 single "The Sound of Silence." I loved the melodic sound of the guitar with the harmonic voices, and I practiced for hours until I learned how to play it and sing both harmonies.

When I recently read the lyrics, I realize now the words reflect how abuse impacts a person's ability to communicate their opinions and feelings. We retreat into the *darkness* of isolation, *softly creep* on eggshells, and don't *dare disturb* the abuser for fear of what they might say or do.

If you've ever been in an abusive situation, you understand how your voice is silenced in a way that doesn't feel emotionally peaceful. I've found that many people who haven't been abused may not understand the feelings you experience, not because they don't care about you but because they can't relate to it.

After my abuse began, I understood food addiction, first as a source of comfort and then as an unhealthy habit. It's still an issue in my life if I'm not careful with boundaries, getting exercise, and eating healthy. I knew what alcohol addiction looked like from my family, but I didn't understand how it felt until I found myself drinking beer in the afternoon and hard alcohol at night almost every day. I thought to myself, *I'm becoming an alcoholic*!

That awareness scared me so much that I immediately stopped drinking beer and only drank hard alcohol maybe once a week. The turning point came when I was confronted by a roommate about drinking one night with my bowling team and then wanting to attend a youth group meeting. She stopped me outside the door and said, "I can smell alcohol. You're not coming in here!" I felt so embarrassed and knew I would be a bad example as a leader to drink at any youth event or anytime I was with them. I went home and later that night made a commitment to her, myself, and God that I would change...and I did.

Food and alcohol addiction slowly entered my life for various reasons, although I didn't realize it at first. I believe for me—and perhaps others reading this book—that abuse happened gradually until it became "normal" and too shameful and difficult to stop.

I think one of the unfortunate and destructive patterns of abuse is that people who commit it and those who receive it may not even know it's happening. As crazy as that may sound, I certainly didn't believe it at first, and I would venture to say some of you reading can relate to that.

What's important to me now, and the main reason I'm writing this book, is to share not only what happened to me, but to bring into the light what I learned about abuse from my experience, research, counseling, and domestic violence support groups. As I said before, I'm not a certified counselor. I understand every relationship is different. My prayer is that at the end of this section, you will know what physical, sexual, verbal, emotional, and financial abuse is and how to identify it and get help if you think it's happening to you or someone you know. There is resource information at the end of this book on where to get help.

The following definitions and behaviors of domestic violence—also known as domestic abuse or spousal abuse—are written as guidelines, so you are knowledgeable of common characteristics. I didn't know that I had been emotionally abused for years until I went to a domestic violence support group at the suggestion of a counselor. I don't want you to suffer as long as I did.

There are endless statistics on domestic violence, and if your partner uses power and control over you, you may be experiencing it. Please know that abuse can occur frequently or occasionally, but in most situations, it gets worse over time and can lead to serious injury or death. People who are abusive are responsible for their behavior and should be held accountable for it. Abuse is <u>never</u> acceptable.

Physical Abuse: Involves using physical force that causes or could cause harm.

Behavior:

- Pushing or shoving
- Slapping
- Kicking
- Pinching
- Choking or strangling
- Punching
- Throwing objects
- Physical restraint (like pinning against a wall, floor, bed, etc.)

- Reckless driving
- Use of weapons.

Sexual Abuse: Threats of unwanted sexual contact or forced sex without consent.

Behavior:

- Rape
- Unprotected sex
- Forcing pornography

Verbal Abuse: Use of words to assault, dominate, ridicule, control, manipulate, or degrade another person that negatively impacts their psychological health.

Behavior:

- Name-calling
- Insults
- Threats
- Belittling
- Sarcasm
- Severe criticism
- Blaming
- Shaming
- Yelling

Emotional Abuse: Pattern of behavior, including verbal abuse, that centers around control, isolation, fear, and strict submission.

Behavior:

- Intimidation
- Isolating from family and friends
- Requires permission for you to go anywhere
- Destroys possessions
- Minimize actions
- Threaten to leave
- Degrade in private but acts charming in public
- Humiliate in private or public
- Withholds appreciation or sex or physical touch as punishment
- Say, "It was just a joke," and that you are too sensitive
- Constantly correct your behavior
- Make you afraid by using gestures or looks
- Name-calling and labels
- Continually have "boundary violations"
- Play the victim to deflect blame
- Remind you of your shortcomings
- Have trouble apologizing

- Threaten to hurt or abuse pets
- Denies they ever used harsh words or did what they are accused of
- Blame you for their behavior.

Financial Abuse: The use of money to control

Behavior:

- Attempts to make someone financially dependent
- Withholds money or credit cards
- Rigidly controls finances
- Requires justification for money spent
- Withholds basic necessities (food, clothes, shelter, medication)
- Harasses you at work
- Steals from you
- Prevents you from working
- Excessive gambling
- Frequent unemployment blaming you or others
- Relying on credit, loans, home equity, family, or government assistance for income instead of getting a job
- Refuses to pay bills/creditors and ruins credit rating.

Every abusive relationship is different. What was true in mine will not be the same for another woman. Abusers do not necessarily exhibit all the behaviors in a particular category. However, if you or someone you know is being abused, you will begin to recognize the unhealthy behavior. What's important is that you identify details of how you are being treated, especially emotionally, as this type of abuse is not as obvious as the physical. If it's abuse, you will begin to see a pattern.

There was a lot of dysfunction in our communication skills that we brought into the marriage. What I learned over the years was not to defend myself. I often told Paul that *he* needed to change but failed to recognize my own issues and work on them. It took me years to finally understand that the only person you can change is yourself!

I confronted Paul many times about his verbal abuse. "I didn't feel loved or respected today at church when you made fun of me in front of our friends," I said.

"When did that happen?" he quickly replied.

"I was answering a question during Sunday school, and you interrupted and joked, 'Patty snores so loud at night, I can't sleep. I'm going to ask Santa for noise-cancelling headphones!'"

His voice got louder. "You do snore, so stop complaining about mine."

"Paul, you interrupted and made fun of me," I cried as tears welled up in my eyes.

"Oh, there you go, starting to cry. You're just too sensitive. 'You made fun of me, Paul,'" he said in a mocking, sing-song voice.

I quickly wiped away the tears. My heart was pounding because I knew where this discussion was probably headed.

"Stop mocking me!" I reacted, raising my voice.

"Stop mocking me," he repeated, starting to laugh.

"I was trying to tell you how I felt today at church. Now you're mocking me. Can't we..."

Paul glared at me as he interrupted, "You're always so critical and judgmental. I knew you had an ulterior motive. You don't accept me. I thought counseling was supposed to help you. You're reverting to your old self. I'm done with this damn conversation, you b**ch!" he said, walking away.

With my head down and shoulders drooping, I slowly walked into my home office. I quietly closed the door, sat down at my desk, and let the tears flow down my face. I reached for the Kleenex and covered my mouth. I tried not to make a sound, afraid Paul would barge in, like he had done so many times in the past, and continue criticizing me. I spent the rest of the evening writing in my journal about what happened, praying that God would make our marriage better, and thinking about how I could change myself. Paul was right that I was sensitive, but I was working on not being critical and judgmental. It was hard work to change; it took time, and my counselor said I was making progress. I was unhappy but didn't know what else to do.

Not until I started tape recording Paul in the middle of an argument did he immediately stop talking and refuse to continue the "discussion" any longer. He wouldn't be able to deny the recording, and I'm sure he was afraid I would play it for our counselor.

There are so many examples I could give of the abuse that happened over the thirty years of marriage. My purpose in writing is not to focus on the problems and point fingers at Paul. I share my experiences, the mistakes I made, and what I learned, to hopefully help others find healthy and successful ways to deal with issues in their relationships. You will need to find what works for your relationship, and get professional help if you're not finding success.

GOD'S PERFECT TIMING

Soon after the abuse started, I found out that the woman Paul was sitting with in church the first time I saw him was from his former church in southern California. That day, he asked her to marry him, and she said, "No." As I probed with questions about how he proposed, I learned the engagement ring he had for her, within six short months, was given to me! When I heard this news, I felt angry to have a "recycled" engagement ring that wasn't chosen especially for me! It seemed like I was a quick second choice to be Paul's wife, especially knowing how fast he proposed to me. I drove to the Golden Gate Bridge and threw the ring over the side into the water! It wasn't a diamond but cubic zirconium—a good analogy of the lower value of what I received in my marriage than what I deserved. The next surprise would reveal Paul's use of control—carefully wrapped in romance—to manipulate me into spending money we didn't have, to get what he wanted.

One night, over a romantic candlelight dinner, Paul said, "I want us to have a second honeymoon. You were working so hard and in school on our first one and deserve to get away now. I want to take you to Europe!"

I was stunned. "Europe? We don't have the money for that!"

"I've got it all figured out. I know about a great discounted tour of France. Then I'll take you to London, and we'll travel the English countryside. Part of the time, we can stay with a great Christian family in England. I know you'll love it!"

Once again, the allure of a new experience, romance, and no responsibility at home got me to say, "Yes." We took an amazing adventure to romantic France and history-rich England. History was one of my strongest subjects in college, and I was in awe to walk inside Notre Dame Cathedral, visit the Eiffel Tower, and gaze from only ten-feet away at the sparkling Crown Jewels.

It seemed that when we traveled, Paul was happier, and we treated each other better—not wanting to ruin our time. Any conflict was quickly resolved, usually by one of us giving in to what the other one wanted. We created a lot of good memories in Europe, on cruise ships, in Hawaii, and during our last major trip together—with eighty people from church—to the Holy Land. The irresponsible part about our traveling was that we were in debt for most of our marriage and yet chose temporary pleasure over long-term financial responsibility. Often on our way home from a nice getaway, the tension would begin to build, and we became critical of each other. I knew that once conflict and arguing followed us on vacations, our effort to make time together enjoyable was losing its importance.

When we got back from Europe, Paul shocked me when he said, "I think it's time for us to try to get pregnant." I jumped up and down and screamed with joy! Paul had wanted us to wait at least two years before I got pregnant so we could have time to do more together. I was now thirty-eight and starting to feel anxious if I would ever have a baby. From that moment, I did everything I knew and could read up on to ensure I was in the best health possible and reduced my stress levels to increase my chances of becoming pregnant.

Weeks and then months went by. My doctor said, "If you're not pregnant next month because of your age, we should start infertility testing." I left his office in tears and prayed God would, once again, fulfill my dream.

The next Sunday, our church was having a dedication of a new altar. Pastor John Bray said, "If you want prayers for anything, please come forward."

I felt a tingling in my body and looked up at Paul, "Let's go up and pray for our baby, if that's God's will for us." He nodded in agreement and held my hand as we walked up together to the altar. Pastor John prayed quietly for us as tears ran down our faces. For the first time, the anxious feeling of wanting a baby left me and was replaced with an unmistakable sense of peace. When we returned to our seats, I whispered to Paul, "Whatever happens, I'll be okay with it."

Three weeks later, I was sitting in the doctor's office, feeling anxious as I waited for him to come in and give me the news. After just a few minutes, my doctor walked in with a big smile. "Congratulations, you're about three weeks pregnant." Tears filled my eyes, and I happily reached out to hug him. My childhood dream was now manifesting itself through a baby. I silently thanked God for the new life that was growing inside me.

Prayer-Thank you, God, for Your perfect timing. You have a plan and purpose for each of us. Help me to reach the woman who needs to hear a message of hope right now. Give her the strength and wisdom to take the first step that will bring peace to her situation.

WE ALL HAVE CHOICES

Have you ever thought to yourself, *I wish I hadn't said that,* or *That wasn't the response I expected,* and vowed never to repeat that mistake again? As imperfect people with unique personalities, we are bound to say or do something that irritates someone. If you have been abused, you know the feeling of being cautious not to upset the abuser. But what I learned over the years is we all have choices on how we respond to situations and people. We can't control or change them, but we can certainly learn to control and change ourselves.

I spent too many years trying to figure Paul out and change him. It would have been best and saved a lot of time and heartache to look at myself and focus on maximizing my strengths and getting help for my hurts, bad habits, and dysfunctional behavior.

It was close to Christmas, and our baby was due in March. I had just finished the laundry and put it on the floor to fold. Paul was watching TV, and I asked him, "Honey, would you fold the laundry when you get a chance?"

"Sure, but I'm watching a good movie. It's almost over."

"Thank you. That's fine." I worked around the house, excited about my baby. An hour later, Paul was still watching TV. He got up to get a drink and then stepped over the laundry to sit in his chair. "When are you going to fold the laundry?" I asked, irritated that he had not started folding the clothes yet.

"You told me there was no rush."

I shook my head and walked out of the room. I began to feel angry as I had been working around the house most of the morning, and he hadn't lifted a finger to help. I realize that people can have different responsibilities in a relationship, where one partner doesn't do the housework but handles something else. In our case, I was six months pregnant and still working full-time. And this wasn't the first time there had been conflict about Paul helping around the house.

"I'm tired of you sitting in front of the TV for hours and not helping me clean the house. You're just lazy!" I blurted out.

He got out of the chair, stepped over the laundry, glared at me, and said, "You fold it."

I was furious and yelled, "You help me!" as I kicked his video tapes across the floor.

He scowled at me, walked over, and shoved me hard onto the floor. I screamed, "Oh dear God. My baby! My baby!"

"You're fine. Stop being hysterical. Leave my tapes alone," he said and walked out of the room. I held back the tears and felt my baby move. I didn't tell anybody, not even my doctor.

When that conflict happened, not only did I keep the physical abuse a secret, but I also didn't work on my perfectionism. I had high expectations of myself. Rather than sit and watch a TV program with my husband, I focused on a clean house. Can anyone relate to that? Of course, Paul could have helped, but yelling at him out of frustration was disrespectful, unproductive, and led to harsh consequences.

"If you stopped criticizing me, or if you treated me with respect, or if you just accepted me, then our relationship would be better, and I wouldn't act that way," Paul said countless times.

When Paul pushed me down in response to whatever he was feeling, especially while I was pregnant, it was not justifiable or acceptable behavior. Abuse <u>never</u> is!

I had a lot of work to do on myself to learn good communication skills, improve my self-esteem, allow others to be themselves, set and maintain boundaries, and make good choices in my relationships. Divorce was not an option in my mind, and I didn't know what it would take to live the dream I had wanted and prayed for since I was a child. Paul was right about me changing, and it would take years and more abuse along the way, but the journey and ultimate outcome was God's plan for me.

My friend, Sandy Russell, is a trauma therapist. This is what she has to say about abuse and some thoughts about what to do.

"I'm sharing with you as someone who has found healing and freedom from the trauma of my own childhood experience with abuse and have been able to help others. Like an onion, I peel back layers, deal with them, and have more freedom. As long as I'm alive, I will continue to heal.

Most of my clients come in with the shame of 'What did I do to <u>cause</u> the abuse?' or 'Why do I <u>continue</u> to let it happen?' or 'Why did I ever <u>allow</u> it to happen?' Part of it is we never think like the perpetrator, could never imagine abusing someone, and may never be able to understand why they did it.

Perpetrators are wounded and don't think like healthy people. They seek out their victims to meet their needs. Often it is by acknowledging the victim's strengths, gifts, compassion, or acting like they can't live without them. Whatever they use to start the relationship, they often get the victim's trust and then hurt them.

What I do know is if you're truly ready for a change and are willing to do the work, I or a good therapist can help you heal through what happened, learn to trust your gut feelings, and not let someone like this in your life again. Clients are often afraid that therapy will bring up everything that they went through. I help you to look at how your body is storing it and affecting you now, help you work through it, know the truth about who you are, and that you don't have to feel like this anymore.

We don't know what your perpetrator will do, and you don't have to know. What's important is to make sure you are safe and learn how to have safe relationships with people who want the best for you and that treat you in the way you deserve. Most of us take on the shame that should be the perpetrator's—not ours—and nothing prepared us for the abuse that happened.

Anytime someone does not want the best for you or wants you to keep something hurtful a secret, that is a signal that something is wrong in the relationship. You need to step back from the relationship, maybe even leave it, and seek help. It is important to learn to take care of yourself and know that self-care is not selfish."

I appreciate Sandy's perspective that we don't need to understand the reasons why our perpetrators abused us in order to get the help we need. What's important is that we recognize something is wrong, understand that the shame is not ours to carry, and with help, can learn how not to let it happen again.

Becoming a mother would be a temporary break from the unhealthy, destructive patterns in my marriage. Two more parts of my dream would come true...I would have a healthy, happy baby and finally move to my dream home. But the journey there was filled with land mines that kept blowing up.

Part 3

WILL OUR RELATIONSHIP EVER CHANGE?

Whether a healthy relationship is possible or not, I have found that the common factor women hold on to is HOPE. We hope that our partner will change. We hope that if we behave like our partner wants us to, the abuse will stop. There is also the hope, especially among faith-based women, that God will do a miracle and we will have the relationship we've longed for.

These were all the basis for my hope that eventually led to the turning point where I was fed up living behind a mask of secrecy, and the relationship changed. You will learn how difficult it was to make the change and the opposition I faced. If you have been abused, you will probably understand most of what I went through and relate it to your own experience. If you haven't been abused, you will gain insight into the dark and hidden secrets many people keep, even those sitting next to you in church and the seemingly happy neighbor.

I was a new mother with a new home and what felt like a new start in our marriage. At forty years old, I was filled with energy and creativity, and God opened new opportunities for our family and future. I also found the HOPE I was searching for in an unexpected way.

MOTHERHOOD, MONEY, AND MIRACLES

After fifteen years of building my career to a successful position in the company, Paul and I agreed that I would quit work to stay home as a full-time mother. He said, "It's a lot of pressure on me, but I have a good job with health and retirement benefits. I wish I could quit and stay home, too!"

Do you know that the number two leading cause for divorce is financial arguments and number one is infidelity? After my first divorce and financial challenges, my mother taught me how to budget. So, I created a written budget for Paul and me before we were married, and I was determined money wouldn't be a source of conflict for us. My unrealistic attitude would lead to many compromises, decisions, and agreements that contributed to our financial problems.

We planned for months to live on just one income. I developed budgeting and debt payoff worksheets, and we set some financial goals. We decided to start Financial Freedom, a money management business to help people get on a budget, pay off debt, and set financial goals. We were active in our church, and God opened opportunities for us.

We saw lives change when people decided and took action to handle money wisely. It seemed reasonable that our business was needed, but the income was less than $500 the first year.

Have you ever agreed to something to make someone happy and afterward realized it was a bad decision? Did you ever do it because you were afraid of conflict? I think many of us who have been abused, even once, make choices that we think will prevent future abuse.

Despite our financial counseling of others, we started a dangerous habit Paul called "creative financing." A few months before Paul Jr. was born, he said, "Let's refinance our condo to pay off most of my debt and get some cash out. It's a good time with lower interest rates."

At first, I said, "No," but he convinced me it would put us in a better position to manage our monthly expenses. Once would have been understandable with a lower interest rate and goal to be out of debt. However, that first decision would lead to refinancing five times, two home equity lines, loans, and credit cards throughout our marriage to cover income shortages and overspending.

The physical abuse had stopped, we enjoyed a lot of family time together with our son, and I loved being a mother. However, baby expenses were more than we anticipated. I will admit, I spoiled our son with toys, name-brand clothes, and whatever I thought would add to his creativity. What's interesting is Paul Jr. acted content with what he had, and I unwisely indulged him with more than he needed. I'm sure part of that was giving him more than I had as a child, but the result was using credit cards.

I'm embarrassed to tell you the truth, but I don't want what happened in the past to have any hold over me because of secrecy. We even went on a cruise and put that on a credit card. There was no accountability with anyone, and nobody knew that the Financial Freedom couple was not financially free at all. I was still wearing a mask of secrecy, but now it was about money.

The price of our condo had doubled in less than five years. We decided to sell it and move to a beautiful new three-bedroom home with a large yard in nearby Petaluma. It was exciting to be in a neighborhood of families with young children, and a few of the mothers stayed home like I did. With a new home comes new expenses, a higher mortgage, and for us, that meant using credit cards. Our Financial Freedom income was only $700 that year, and we were adding business expenses.

One quality I learned about Paul after we married was that he wanted to be self-employed and not work a 9–5 job. His dream job was to be a singer, and I encouraged him to sing, but I still wanted him to focus on having a full-time job.

In December, Paul had a low-performance appraisal and was put on probation. He blamed his work environment and quit his job. I felt anxious about his decision, lost sleep at night, and worried about how we would pay our bills. We withdrew a large sum of money from our IRAs to help with expenses.

With Paul being home full-time, our business income increased, but it was only $3,400 that year. We argued about money and blamed each other for the rapidly increasing debt. The cycle of Paul's violent anger, followed by empty apologies, started again with him hitting and shoving me. We called each other names, and I believed him when he said that my critical remarks caused his loss of control. I felt insecure and focused my attention on nurturing my child.

Paul Jr. was only four, and I protected him from hearing or seeing any verbal or physical abuse. I looked for happiness in activities with my son, taking him shopping at Toys-R-Us, fun outings at the zoo and aquarium, and play dates with my friends and their children. There was Sunday school and kids' events at church for him, and I often volunteered to teach and play the guitar.

Almost two years later, Paul started working full-time again. I agreed to another terrible financial decision to take out an equity loan on our home with our commitment that, "We will only use it for *emergencies.*" Does that sound familiar to anyone? Emergencies turned into new clothes, house décor, and "need to have" vacations. We paid down our $25,000 debt, but our spending habits kept us from saving for emergency expenses.

Over the next two years, even with Paul working, our Financial Freedom business began to grow. An article came out on the front page of the local newspaper about our success with clients, despite our personal financial struggles. Our embarrassment of sharing about our debt, and efforts to pay it off, turned into joy and gratefulness when we saw the impact on people.

God used our public vulnerability to open the doors for us to teach thousands of people how to budget, set financial goals, and get out of debt. There were interviews on TV and radio. Several churches hired us for weekend seminars, we spoke at conferences, and people signed up for individual counseling. I started women's Bible studies and workshops and invited guest speakers to talk about investing and planning for widowhood. There were tears of joy when we heard about marriages being saved and people escaping the bondage of debt. We were in awe hearing "money miracles" about unexpected $10,000 checks in the mail and $15,000 business loans paid off within a week of trusting God for income.

I joined a speaking program called Toastmasters to improve my speaking skills. I quickly advanced to leadership roles. At a conference, I was asked to introduce the keynote speaker, Patricia Fripp, a well-known and award-winning speaker and sales trainer.

Ms. Fripp asked me, "Patricia, would you help me at my product table during breaks?"

"Yes!" I quickly said.

At the end of the very busy sales, Ms. Fripp, who later told me to call her, "Fripp" said, "I'm doing a seminar next week in San Francisco. Would you like to help me, and I'll pay you?"

"Let me think about it...yes!!!"

During the week, I studied her website and found a few spelling and grammar mistakes. I sent her an email informing her, "You may want your webmaster to correct these." I had also taken her handwritten price sheets home and developed a printed reference form with each product, price, tax, and total to speed up processing sales. Fripp was pleased with my initiative.

At her seminar, there was a book I wanted to purchase. She said, "I am impressed with your work. I'm revising that book. How would you like to proofread it for me?"

I was speechless! In college, I had excellent grades in English and was good with details. I don't know how long I stared at Fripp in complete shock. "Yes, I would love to!" I finally said.

That was the beginning of my proofreading business. Over twenty-five years later, it has developed into PL Creative Editing. Fripp has referred me to many successful and influential people, including her famous brother, legendary guitarist Robert Fripp. She taught me speaking skills that have helped me be a better editor, gave me fascinating projects to work on, and has consistently been a generous source of income over the years. She is a priceless part of my business and life. When you go through traumatic experiences like I have, it's a blessing to have someone like Patricia Fripp there for you.

Less than two years after starting his full-time job, Paul quit. That night after Paul Jr. went to bed, we were sitting on the couch getting ready to watch a romantic movie. He smiled, took my hand, and said, "God has blessed our business, and you're bringing in proofreading income. I want to build Financial Freedom and start doing more singing gigs."

I let go of his trembling hand, glared at him, and said sternly, "Yes, I'm getting more clients, and God has blessed our business. I do most of the work, and you just show up for a client meeting or seminar. You don't even want to practice our talks that *I've* written."

"Wow, thanks for the encouragement," he responded sarcastically. "You think you're better than me, being in Toastmasters. I don't need it to prepare what I already know."

"You could certainly use it the way you ramble," I snapped back. "We were just getting out of debt and…"

"You're always worried about money," he scowled at me. "You don't accept me or believe in me. How do you expect me to be attracted to you? You give more attention to Paul than to me!" I was quiet as tears started to roll down my face. "Don't start to cry. You do that to manipulate me."

He jumped off the couch and snarled, "I'm going to bed, and in the morning, I'm going to the gym. Enjoy the romantic movie by yourself. You ruined it for us."

I heard him slam the bedroom door. I got up and quietly opened Paul Jr.'s door. He was sound asleep. I closed the door, went to the couch, and cried uncontrollably. I felt hopeless about our marriage and anxious that our savings would soon be gone, leaving us in debt again.

We took more money out of our IRAs and borrowed money from my parents. Within a year, our business was declining and Paul began teaching basic computer classes at local companies and the junior college several times a month.

A year later, he got another full-time job, but it involved an hour commute each way by bus to San Francisco. He slept on the bus, liked his job, but there was not much family time after dinner, or for him and me to be alone together, before he wanted to go to sleep.

Although I was satisfied Paul was working, I had migraines and trouble sleeping. I worried about paying the bills, how long he would keep his job, and when all the fighting in our marriage would end. Why couldn't I relax more and not worry so much? I was praying for God's help, but I know now that He was waiting for me to get the help I needed and make the choice to change. I heard once that God takes care of the birds, but He doesn't drop the worms in their nest. God would do His part, but I had to be responsible for mine. Paul needed to be responsible for his part, and it was not up to me to change him, but I tried.

I started my long journey of change. During this time period, I met with a women's ministry leader from church who offered to mentor me. I felt encouraged and safe talking with her. After a few weeks, and a lot of prayer for God's help, I had the courage to share about the verbal and physical abuse. My heart was pounding, my hands shaking, and tears streamed down my face. My mentor and I talked, prayed together, and I felt understood and safe.

I learned to set a few boundaries, express my feelings more openly, and not criticize Paul as often. After an outburst, he agreed to meet with a guy from church and get professional help for his anger issues. I had hope that our marriage would improve, and that year there was less abuse.

I'll never forget that spring when Paul Jr. attended his first wedding. It was in a beautiful church with stained glass windows, and an organ that filled the room with melody as the bride walked down the long aisle. "Mommy," Paul whispered, "it's a prince and princess getting married." The spiritually-focused ceremony kept his attention.

Afterwards, my son's eyes opened wide, and a smile covered his face when he met and shook the hand of the handsome prince. He shyly looked down when the beautiful princess said, 'I'm so happy to meet you, Paul." That evening, he said to me, "Mommy, I want to ask Jesus into my heart." With tears in my eyes, I held his tiny hand and prayed with him. It was the beginning of his own personal relationship with God.

Little did I know that nine years later, the groom's brother, Greg, would baptize my son in the presence of several people who were there at the wedding. Over the years, Paul's Christian faith would be vital in helping him with the issues and trauma he would experience, surviving a near-fatal car accident, showing my son the purpose God had for him in music, and leading him to his wife, Kelly.

Paul Jr. attended a Christian school, got an excellent education, and learned the foundational teachings of the Bible. It was the best investment in his early childhood development that we made. I taught my son to play the guitar and enrolled him in piano lessons.

He played on a few sports teams and wanted to learn to play golf with his friend, Josh. I drove Paul Jr. around to so many lessons and tournaments I finally said, "I'm here at the course so much, I might as well learn to play!"

Although Paul wasn't interested, I finally convinced him to try golf. We bought him clothes, shoes, and golf clubs. He didn't want to take lessons, complained that golf was too expensive, and quit.

I felt disappointed that we couldn't enjoy it as a family and told Paul, "You're missing out on time with your son." It became an activity for Paul Jr. and I to share for years, and golf is now my favorite sport.

Our marriage suffered from ongoing conflicts. We went to counseling, marriage seminars, read books, signed agreements to reinforce promises we made about money and Paul's job search, and became accountable to others. A spiritually mature couple at church counseled us for months. And with our seven-year-old son and pastor as witnesses, we recommitted our marriage vows and relationship to God. I had hope our marriage would change.

Typically, any behavior change is temporary. Permanent change takes commitment, discipline, and a lot of work. The reality is that we can only change ourselves.

People don't change unless they choose to. The honeymoon was over in a few weeks, and the reality of life returned.

I felt guilty spending money, especially on myself, and I turned to comfort from a source I could justify buying...food. I had been in excellent health after Paul was born, and unhealthy and overeating had never been a problem my entire life. My food addiction, like all harmful habits, started slowly to comfort me after an argument, relieved my stress from worrying about money, and give me a false sense of control over a situation when the reality was that I was out of control.

I started to isolate myself and learned to suppress my feelings of anger, mistrust, and resentment to avoid conflict. God was still with me, but I tried to control everyone and everything as a solution to the battles going on around me.

Hiding my overeating was emotionally shameful, physically harmful, and spiritually sinful. I tried different ways to get back to my normal ways of thinking and eating, but over the next ten years, I gained forty pounds. I look back at photos and see a smile on my face, but I know there was deep anger, worry, and sadness inside.

Just when I had almost lost hope our marriage would change, we would ever get out of debt, or I would live in my dream home, God showed us mercy and generosity one more time.

Paul left his job in San Francisco when he was hired by one of the most successful technology companies in the world. He had valuable stock options, excellent health and retirement benefits, and income that brought our net worth over a million dollars. He was well respected as a systems trainer and used his education and experience in a job he enjoyed.

One day, Paul Jr. and I visited my husband during lunch at work which was just ten minutes from our home. My son's eyes got huge, and a big smile spread across his face when Paul said, "All the food is free, including the candy in those vending machines!" Paul Jr. went home with pockets full of candy, and I stuck Snickers bars in my purse.

Paul needed to be with the company a year before the stock options would be vested and permanently ours. The value would set us up for a comfortable retirement. I was in awe of how God had blessed us, despite our hurtful behavior and frequent financial mistakes. Paul and I were happy together, had less conflict, and I believed God had answered my prayers for change. Even Paul Jr. seemed to be doing well in school, played guitar and piano, and was happy with his puppy named Max.

Eight months later, the technology bubble burst, and so did my dream when Paul's company was hit hard. I felt blindsided by this sudden crash, and Paul was among thousands of workers who lost their jobs. Although he got a severance package, his stock options were gone. I was thankful there was no credit card debt, but the money in our savings account soon disappeared.

A man's identity is often tied to his job. The loss of this dream job crushed Paul's identity. My security of having money was shattered too. The next eight months were emotionally hard for both of us, with only a few outbursts of abuse that we kept hidden from our son. We again took money out of our IRAs.

God was faithful to us, and nine months later, Paul got a great job with Wells Fargo Mortgage. I was so proud of him with the service he provided, how clients praised him, and the company significantly rewarded him for his hard work. Refinancing homes was booming, and Paul benefitted big time. We started putting money in savings, and the physical abuse stopped.

Within eight months, Paul had another "creative financing" idea. He was paid commissions on refinances, and our monthly mortgage payment was high. There were new "adjustable" mortgages where we only had to pay interest and whatever principle we wanted. It sounded financially unstable but significantly improved our cash flow. I agreed, Paul was happy, and there was breathing room in our budget.

The financial trap we had fallen into as a result of decisions to choose temporary relief over long-term responsibility had consequences. After two refinances and ten years of monthly payments, our mortgage was $37,000 higher than when we moved in! They say insanity is doing the same thing over and over and expecting different results. We were six months away from making an insane choice that would be part of God's plan to fulfill my dream, but in the process, show me His greater purpose for my life.

If you've been abused, you understand how new beginnings can give you HOPE for your relationship and an opportunity to change your future. I believed an answer to my prayers and childhood dream would soon bring a breakthrough in our marriage.

MY DREAM HOME AND A NEW START

Do you have a friend or two who you talk to and never feel judged, even with your darkest secrets? Have they helped you through any challenges in life? Friendships have been the greatest blessing in my journey of recovery from abuse and my dysfunctional issues. One of those friends is Marlene, and she and her family were unknowingly influential in finding my dream home.

We were good friends with her family when we lived in Petaluma. Our children got along well, and Marlene's son Evan influenced Paul Jr.'s interest in music, specifically the guitar. When they moved to the Sacramento area, we visited them, went to church together, and often stayed at their beautiful home. We were in awe of how low housing prices were, and they kept saying, "You should move here!" The bonus was Ray Johnston, the youth pastor I was friends with from Marin Covenant Church, was now the pastor of a thriving new church called Bayside.

One weekend on our way home from nearby Lake Tahoe, Marlene said, "Why don't you let Paul Jr. spend a couple of days with us?" It sounded like a great idea to everyone.

During the drive home to Petaluma, I said to Paul, "Why don't we start looking closer at homes there? Ours has significantly appreciated, and we could sell it, pay off our mortgage and equity line, and with the profit get a new larger home with a low mortgage and have a lot of money left over." I was beginning to sound like Paul!

"I could transfer to Wells Fargo up there and get us a low mortgage rate!" Paul said.

Two days later when I picked Paul Jr. up, we stopped at a couple of new neighborhoods. My teenage son stayed in the car to rest while I looked at model homes. The last stop was in Roseville. I took one look at the model, the price, and came running out to the car. "Paul, wake up! Come in to look. I want to know what you think." Most teenage boys would rather text on their phones than look at model homes with their mothers, but Paul agreed.

"That's a big house," Paul Jr. said as we walked to the car. "I could have my friends over to play Xbox in the family room. The yard's big enough for a pool."

With those confirming comments, I said, "Yes!!" and we jumped in the car. I felt overcome with joy, and with tears starting to fall, I closed my eyes and said, "Thank you, Lord for answering my prayers." I immediately called Paul, "I found *our* dream home! It's four bedrooms, a large kitchen overlooking the family room, beautiful living room, and Paul Jr. likes it! I'm sure the finances will work out well for us, and it's only a mile from Bayside Church!" Mind you, this was only the model, not the actual one we could buy.

Paul's response was subdued, compared to the enthusiasm he showed two days earlier. In a monotone voice, he said, "We'll talk about it when you get home."

"Okay. I think God is telling me this is the neighborhood, but I'll prepare budgets for us."

I called the Roseville model homes to find out the costs of the home. Paul and I argued over the type of mortgage we should get. I wanted a 30-year fixed rate, and he insisted the adjustable rate would make our payments lower and help with cash flow. I finally gave in when I heard the words, "I know what I'm doing. You need to trust me." I went to the kitchen and ate to relieve my stress and fight off the headache that was starting.

I created different budgets for us to stay in Petaluma or move to Roseville. I determined how long it would take to pay off our debts. How much income we needed to meet monthly expenses in both homes. Expenses to sell our home and projected move-in expenses of the new home, including landscaping and the possibility of a pool. I addressed every financial angle I could think of. To say I was obsessive about the money is an understatement! This might be my dream home, but I was going to be sure we could afford it.

Our discussion became tense when we sat down a few days later to discuss our possible move. "My work at Wells Fargo is slowing down. I'm only getting commissions on new home sales, not refinances," Paul said. "I called Wells Fargo in Roseville, and they have an opening, but I won't be paid as much there."

My heart sank. I had been through multiple job losses, with long stretches without income. What if Paul lost his job? How would we pay our mortgage?

"I don't want to risk moving with an unknown income. At least people know us here, you can work at Wells Fargo, do some singing gigs, I've got proofreading income, and our expenses won't increase," I knew my dream was quickly fading.

"I have an idea! Paul blurted out. "We can refinance our home, get an equity line to help with the mortgage down payment on the Roseville home, and rent out this home at a net profit to bring in more income. Home values are going up, and in a year, we can sell this home for a huge profit, then, use that money to pay down the new mortgage, and have cash left over. It makes total sense, and you can get your dream home." Seemed like Paul had thought this through before we even talked.

"But what about your job?"

"Patty, where is your faith in God to provide? You don't trust me to keep my job. Haven't I brought home a lot of money? I think there's more of a spending problem."

At that point, I knew the conversation was going downhill and didn't want the conflict to escalate. I felt guilty for spending more money than we budgeted, and I didn't trust him to keep a job for more than a year. I thought I had a strong faith in God to provide because of all the "money miracles" I had seen over the years. I just didn't know for sure if God wanted us to move and how the income would work out. But then again, God always took care of our needs.

"Let me think about your idea of renting this home. I want to run some numbers."

I felt a little better seeing in black and white how renting, refinancing, and an equity line could help us buy the home. The missing piece, of course, was the guaranteed income we would need. The frightening part was a large open line of credit that had money available whenever we wanted it, even if the reason wasn't an emergency or valid need. This easy money had been, in some cases, irresponsibly used the first time we got a credit line. There was no history that this time would be any different.

A few days later, we sat down to talk. "Your idea could work, Paul, but I'm concerned about the large equity line and the money you will have to bring in every month. That seems like it may put a lot of pressure on you."

"You still don't trust me. Stop worrying so much," Paul pleaded. "The equity on this home continues to go up. The money is sitting there available to us. When we sell the house, we'll pay the credit line off and have money left over. As the head of this family, I am responsible for the final decision. I think it is a wise decision."

The conversation went back and forth about details of how to rent, what if we got a bad tenant, Paul Jr. changing schools as a seventh grader in the middle of the year, and leaving all our friends and my family who lived nearby. Paul Jr. walked in, and I told him some of the financial details and about going to a new school and church. "How do you feel about moving?"

"I think it's more than you can afford. That doesn't mean we shouldn't move. We need to trust God to have a plan. Dad, you need to keep your job. I already have friends at church with Scott and Mark Johnston. I'll be okay at school. Mom, you really want this house. I know it will make you happy."

I was so proud of the level of maturity in his answer. He was sensitive to what he had seen and heard in our home, but even as a teenager showed leadership qualities in conflict resolution. This wouldn't be the last time our son would be in a position to give advice to his dad and me.

I danced with excitement as we got in the car and drove just over an hour to Roseville. We chose the home we wanted built, including the neighborhood location, carpeting, and kitchen accessories. Paul seemed bored, but I was thrilled to feel creative. He perked up when we met our neighbors, and everyone seemed friendly and happy.

We refinanced, got our equity line, and put a down payment on our home. On one hand, I felt happy about what I envisioned our new home would look like. I was stressed and overwhelmed with all the financial papers. Getting our house ready to rent was a monumental project. The packing seemed endless along with sorting items to sell, donate, or throw away. I felt resentful that Paul didn't help me more, but I wanted to avoid conflict...so I ate instead.

God took care of our renting worries when a friend who managed rentals immediately found a military couple who always paid their rent on time and kept our home in better shape than we did. I believed God had the best plan for us, and it wasn't my job to figure everything out. That included how to deal with Paul's decreasing income and my increasing frustration. When I wanted something done, I was often critical, impatient, and controlling. The Bible says in Proverbs 21:9, "Better to live on a corner of the roof than share a house with a quarrelsome wife." Thank goodness I've changed, but I would have made a good drill sergeant in the Army!

I was singing and happy on the drive up to sign our papers and get the keys to our dream home. We were almost there when Paul said, "You know I haven't been making a lot of money at Wells Fargo. They're not very supportive to help me with leads to clients, so I quit my job." I felt like I had just been punched in the stomach.

"What?!! You quit without even telling me ahead of time? We're going to sign our papers, and you don't have a job."

"Calm down. I got a job with a mortgage company that will pay higher commissions. I have training next week on company procedures and will start getting clients the following week."

"Do they give you leads?"

"Well, not exactly. The company is growing and needs more people. They do a lot of business in this area."

I felt betrayed, manipulated, and angry. I was quiet and held back the tears as I stared out the window, and neither of us talked. We signed the papers and got the keys. Rather than feeling happy about my dream home and celebrating, I felt empty inside.

On the way home, Paul tried to convince me that he would do well on this new job, but I didn't believe him. I thought about the equity line and how long it would last. Thankfully, Paul Jr. wasn't home. Paul left the house to go to the gym. I isolated myself in our room and cried. I asked God, "Why? I thought this was Your plan. I don't know what to do now. Please help me." I didn't tell anyone, especially my parents, who had financially helped us several times.

Friends and family helped us move, and it was a good day. Our new neighbors waved and said hello. The warm sunshine coming through the windows seemed to promise this would be a new start. As I stood daydreaming about how to make our new house a home, the sound of the doorbell got my attention.

A young boy stood at our door. "Hi, I'm Nikko. I saw your son walking around. Can he come play at our house down the street?"

I smiled, "Sure, Nikko. I'm Mrs. Lauterjung." The two boys ran off together, and my heart warmed. God did have a plan, and the timing was perfect.

We attended Bayside Church, a thriving fellowship with opportunities for spiritual growth and a fabulous youth group for our teenage son. One day driving home from church, Paul Jr. said, "Mom, I love going to church!" He would soon meet his best friend, Ean, who to this day I refer to as Son #2. Paul and I were in a small group, two of the couples lived in our neighborhood, and Paul Jr. went to the youth group and school with one of the boys. I co-led a women's Bible study and presented women's workshops on money management. Paul and I were actively involved in church, including a fabulous group for married couples. There I would meet one of my closest friends, Wendy, who would become one of my greatest supporters during the darkest and hardest hours of my life.

I truly believed this move was a new beginning for our marriage, and God's favor seemed to be on us, despite the potholes along the path He was leading us on. Over the next four months, Paul started and lost three jobs and then was out of work for almost a year. We used our equity line to live on. I got a part-time job working in the Finance Department at Bayside and loved making new friends, being in the center of the action of this dynamic church, and gained confidence using my education and work experience.

"I know a lot of people at church," I told Paul Jr. "So, you better behave with all those eyes on you," I laughed. When you're friends with Pastor Johnston's sons, there is bound to be shenanigans, and there was. I was thankful for the long-time friendship we had with Ray and Carol Johnston.

After a year, our excellent renters were being transferred to Germany. We sold our Petaluma home, which had doubled in price, paid off the mortgage and two equity lines, and had an incredible profit. One evening after we had finished dinner, I reluctantly approached Paul. "God has provided a miracle and an opportunity for us to pay off our new home in less than ten years. I want to tithe and give ten percent of the profit and then use most of it to pay down our mortgage and refinance to a fixed rate." Paul agreed to tithe, which had been our commitment since we were married, but refused to put profit toward our mortgage or refinance. There was nothing I could say to change his mind.

We put in a pool, hot tub, and landscaping and went on vacation to Hawaii and Lake Tahoe. We enjoyed our new home, friends, church, and the Sacramento area. But with Paul not working and the ongoing habit of living beyond our means, in less than a year, the entire profit was gone.

The physical abuse started again with hitting and pushing me against walls. We started counseling again, but it seemed as soon as we left the office, there was no change. I continued to pray that God would change our marriage and believed He could do a miracle. I lost and gained weight and was critical of Paul.

During this time, our son spent more time with his friends away from our home. I tried to make our home a place for Paul Jr.'s friends to hang out, swim, play video games, and have sleepovers. I enjoyed the boys being there, and Paul was on better behavior when they were around. Nobody knew, except our son, to a certain extent, the depth of our dysfunctional behavior and harsh words. I was worried about the effect on him, but he seemed to be enjoying life as a normal teenage boy, was taking guitar lessons, and was active in church.

When our house-sale profit ran out, and credit card debt increased, Paul got a job as an insurance salesman. There were a lot of good leads for new clients, and he won a romantic cruise for us to Puerto Rico. The additional income made us feel better, and we agreed it was okay to quit my job at Bayside. I still had my proofreading business and was occasionally paid for speaking engagements and financial counseling I did for women.

After about a year of pressure being on Paul to meet quotas, the leads started dying down, and our debt was still high. We began to argue more about money. I was learning the pattern of our behavior and the consequences of unwise financial decisions. I refused to take out another equity line against our home. I was trusting God to provide for our basic needs and for us to do our part to be financially responsible. Paul was angry, but I wouldn't give in to the pressure to take the easy way out. I also didn't know how long he would keep this job, the twelfth in eighteen years of marriage. We had no significant retirement savings or future pensions except the two small ones from my jobs before we were married and Paul's IRA he set up from the house-sale profit. I was fifty-five years old, and my life was not the dream of living happily ever after.

We couldn't pay our income taxes, and the interest on our credit cards alone was over $200. To help bring in income, but more importantly, to be with my loving ninety-year-old mother, I did a lot of financial work and helped her in a variety of ways after Dad passed away. She was paying me, and I started putting a little of it aside for myself. I can still hear her voice, "Patricia, you need to take care of yourself."

Paul was upset that I had my own money, but I didn't care because I knew I was managing all the bills, financial paperwork, and doing the majority of the work around the house. To help with income, I got a part-time job as an administrative assistant for two of the top producing agents at the insurance company where Paul worked. It became a source of conflict and continual arguments. I frequently gave him unsolicited advice on actions I observed them take to earn money and win awards. I told him what he needed to do to change, and rationalized my attitude and behavior as "helping him" to be more successful.

My lack of respect for my husband's self-esteem as a man hurt Paul, and it contributed to the damage in our relationship. I'm ashamed to admit that I set up a pattern of controlling behavior based on fear and insecurity of not having enough money to pay bills. I had seen God provide for our basic needs and more, despite our spending habits. I prayed that God would change Paul, instead of focusing on what transformation God wanted for *me*.

My dysfunctional behavior only enabled Paul's behavior not to change. As his insurance sales income continued to drop, his boss told him he expected better performance. In addition, I put more pressure on him to change. The stress led to emotional and physical reactions in Paul. He felt inadequate and was impatient with me spending money on golf, too many groceries, and music lessons for our son. He was diagnosed with a sleeping disorder called sleep apnea, and felt self-conscious wearing a breathing mask at night. He experienced stomach problems to certain foods. I grew impatient and frustrated, feeling like I was a nurse to someone who would get better, only if he changed his behavior.

Without warning, Paul suddenly developed a serious voice problem called spasmodic dysphonia. It caused breathing issues when he spoke, and his voice was raspy. Over a period of several years, a multitude of doctors and medical experts couldn't heal him. He felt frustrated trying to talk to people, especially insurance clients. The surprising part was, his voice sounded wonderful when he sang! But if he talked between songs, the inarticulate rasping immediately returned. I felt compassion for Paul, and was less controlling, and more encouraging of who he was and what he tried to do to bring in income.

With Paul's medical issues, decreasing income, and our mounting debt from using credit cards, I agreed to refinance our home. Lower monthly payments helped our cash flow, but our mortgage was $40,000 higher than when we moved in. My expectation of where we would be financially after twenty years of marriage and ten years until retirement was not a $335,000 mortgage and being $40,000 in debt. I felt discouraged, lost sleep at night, and my migraines returned. The more I tried to control what was happening, the worse my situation seemed to get.

Paul felt discouraged about his voice and was stressed from the pressure on his job. Like me, he was eating more, but we both continued to go to the gym for exercise. One evening after dinner, Paul said with hesitation, "I made an important decision for us today. I know you've been worried about our debt, like I have, and we don't have money to pay our income taxes. I closed out my IRA that we opened when we sold our Petaluma house."

"You did what?" I demanded as I glared at him.

"You heard me. I cashed out my IRA to help us," he said, reaching in his pocket and shoving the receipt toward me.

I was furious when I saw $2,000 in fees and almost $3,000 in taxes for early withdrawal. "Why didn't you talk to me first? That was a stupid decision!"

He scowled at me, and in a clear, loud voice replied, "You don't appreciate anything I do! I was trying to help you not to worry. All you care about is money. I'm done with this conversation." He got up from the table and walked out the front door, slamming it behind him.

Once again, I felt blindsided by a decision I had not been part of but that affected me. I felt betrayed and didn't know what to do to prevent what felt like an avalanche of debt coming down on me.

Paul was soon let go from his job, and he blamed me for not supporting him with encouragement. He withdrew from me physically, and I started sleeping in the guest bedroom. The debt continued to grow, and the physical abuse returned. The verbal abuse felt worse than being shoved or hit because it was almost every day and often an attack on my character. My self-esteem was shattered, and I felt like a prisoner in what was supposed to be my dream home. I still didn't tell anyone about the abuse and put on a smile when I walked out my door.

Although my brother, Richard, didn't know about the abuse, he heard about our financial problems and knew Paul was in and out of jobs. My brother is one of the hardest working guys I know, and he and his wife Amanda are very responsible with money. Richard used tough love to help me do what I couldn't for myself:

- Stop making irresponsible financial decisions.

- Cut up our credit cards.

- Stop borrowing money from my mother.

- Eliminate unnecessary expenses, and

- Stop agreeing to Paul's ideas to access our home equity to cover no job.

Every month I sent Richard a written budget that showed our income, expenses, and any shortage for the next month. Knowing that he would see where money was spent brought out the frugal side of me and strict food and spending boundaries.

Richard was tough on Paul. My once proud husband had to humble himself and apply for government assistance (known as EBT food stamps), get any kind of job available, and send a written weekly report on job status to Richard, which was surprisingly motivating to Paul. He even started cutting our lawn instead of paying for it.

In return for these humbling and strict commitments on our part, for the next six months, my brother wrote checks for any monthly deficits, paid off our credit cards, and paid past-due income and property taxes. It was a significant amount of money. We signed agreements for these loans with a commitment to start paying Richard back when Paul got a full-time job, and any balance due would be paid out of my inheritance when my mother passed away.

Our spending behavior changed; we both looked for ways to increase our income. We made do with what we had and stayed home more. It was difficult to change years of habits, and the stress led again to abuse.

One day, Paul Jr. confronted both of us for fighting. "You need to be in counseling and stop criticizing each other so much. You act one way at church and another way at home."

This shocked both of us. Paul Jr. was right. He was nineteen years old now and very mature for his age. He didn't complain about having less, but showed by working and saving money that, despite what he saw at home, our son was becoming financially responsible. Paul Jr. wasn't perfect, but he learned to make better choices from our mistakes.

The week of Christmas, Paul got a call that he was hired for a great job with the State of California! It was a good fit for his experience, with fabulous health and retirement benefits and a beautiful location near the Sacramento State Capitol. We hugged and kissed. "I'm so proud of you, honey. God has answered our prayers and hard work. This is a new beginning."

"Yes, He has. We need to let go of the past and move forward," Paul smiled.

We continued with the couples and individual counseling, stayed involved at church, and got our finances in much better shape. There was still conflict in our marriage, but the security of a steady job lightened the tension.

Why am I letting you in on all this personal, financial, and relationship information? I want the woman who is being abused to know she's not alone. There are many others who stay in a relationship believing God, the universe, or something outside of themselves will change it and stop the abuse. We think that the key is having more money, a bigger home, a baby, a successful job, or even a happy partner. I had all those things, and yet, the abuse continued.

GETTING THE HELP I NEED

Have you ever thought to yourself...*I wish that person would change! Their attitude stinks. They are such a hypocrite. I'm tired of always being the one who apologizes. What happened is not my fault, and I'm going to prove it. Our relationship would be so much better if they got counseling.* Maybe you don't relate to any of those statements, but that was me for most of our marriage.

Blaming others started with me saying, "I didn't do it. Richard did!" Over the years, I had a hard time taking responsibility for my actions and sometimes lied to cover for my guilt. I blamed Paul for why I gained weight, our increasing debt, and my being a workaholic. Yes, he was responsible for his actions, but I had choices on my own behavior. I acted like a miserable victim. I blamed my cheating ex-husband from forty years ago, my boss, who took credit for my work thirty-five years ago, and the sixth-grade girl who bullied me.

I have prayed out loud these words almost every time I sit down to write, "Lord, help me to say what You want. I need You. Please be with me. We're in this together."

Just before I started writing this chapter, I was looking at testimonials of recovery I had written seven, eight, and nine years ago. I glanced at books I had studied to help me change and had written down so many feelings, experiences, and secrets. I texted a friend who's been praying for me, "I'm beginning the chapter on getting help. I'm looking at papers, and what I wrote is upsetting. It was such a hurtful time, but the good results speak for themselves. I know there will be healing in this; I just need to go through it. The Lord is with me...."

She texted back, "Absolutely. Love you. So hard. You're not alone and free now to share your truth."

Jesus says in John 8:31-32, "If you follow my teaching, you will know the truth, and the truth will set you free." On March 11, 2011, I took the first step to change the unhealthy direction of my life and would find freedom from so many issues I had never resolved.

Paul and I were on a mini-retreat in an empty room at the church to work on our marriage. We couldn't afford to go with the Bayside couples group to beautiful Napa. We had taken Community Care Pastor Mark's wise suggestion to redirect our money towards more counseling. He knew about our marriage problems and critical financial position. Yet, he felt we were on the verge of a significant breakthrough. Little did he know that God had something life-changing in mind that was about to happen on our retreat.

During Paul's and my "heated" discussion, a guy looked in the door and said, "Is this where the anger management group is meeting?"

"No, I don't think so," I replied with a puzzled look.

Another guy looked in, then a third, and the fourth one said, "Sorry, I thought this room was the anger management group."

I laughed and looked at Paul, "Why do they think we need anger management? Maybe we better leave."

We walked downstairs into the middle of a meeting. A woman was sharing her testimony about finding freedom from anger and drug addiction and the positive effect it had on her marriage. I was curious about what she was saying, but quickly felt tense and irritated when Paul decided to go over to the church café instead of listening to the speaker. It was obvious to me that _he_ needed to hear this! After all, he had an anger problem, not me.

I stayed for the next hour to hear others talk openly about how Christ had freed them from their bad habits, negative emotions, and addictions. I thought, *I am so unhappy, fed up with my marriage, and tired of acting like I'm okay.*

In that moment, God clearly, but gently spoke into my thoughts, "You need to be here."

I came back the next Friday night, angry again that Paul wasn't with me. I was breathing hard and embarrassed walking into the meeting alone. *People are going to think I'm an alcoholic or use drugs. That's what this group is about.* I avoided eye contact and sat in the back. After worship with singing, which I loved, and a lesson that spoke directly to me on how to overcome feelings of failure, I met with a few women who were also there for the first time. When it came to my turn to share why I was there, I said, "I don't have an issue with alcohol or drugs, but I'm having marriage problems." Other women nodded their heads, and I got tears in my eyes. Somehow, I felt understood and not alone.

I found out that Celebrate Recovery (CR) is a Christ-centered, twelve-step recovery program that provides support to men and women who struggle with any type of addiction, hurt, or habit. It is a safe place to work through issues that affect your life with weekly teaching, worship, fellowship, and small group support called a Step Study.

Each week I went to a meeting, I was surprised how some talked openly about their problems. I didn't want them to know too much about me. I had secrets about my past and family. I thought if they knew about my sinful behavior and the problems we had in our marriage, they wouldn't like me. I talked about my son and Paul...and cried. It was the first time that I could remember that nobody interrupted me, gave me advice, or criticized me for crying. I kept coming back and found I wasn't alone in my feelings or experiences. I continued to cry, and nobody gave advice or criticized me. Despite what I shared, the ladies were friendly and seemed to like me.

If you've ever been in a recovery program like Celebrate Recovery or Alcoholics Anonymous, you know the importance of confidentiality. When people share about being kicked by their partner, taking meth and other drugs to escape their pain, and relapsing with alcohol, they need to feel safe that no one in the room will walk out and tell their neighbor. If anyone was found gossiping, they were asked to leave CR and not come back.

If you're reading this and haven't told anyone, for whatever reason, about what abuse has happened to you, please know there is help. If you are in danger, please call your local police department. They will also help you with community support services. You can Google *domestic violence* for local, state, and national assistance. I have included a Resource section in the back of this book. Thousands of people are hurt or killed each year by their spouses or partners. Please take care of yourself...and your children.

After a month of the group meetings, I decided to join what's called a Step Study group. There were ten women in mine, and I made a commitment to be there every Monday night for a year, and God showed up every week!

If you had trust, anger, and abuse issues like I did, you can imagine it took weeks for me to open up and say, "My husband grabbed my wrists yesterday and pushed me up against a wall." When I saw tears and nods from other women, I knew they were not just feeling bad for me. They understood my fear because it was theirs as well.

The two leaders in the group, Linda and Marie, kept us focused on ourselves and not blaming others. More than once, they interrupted me with a stark reminder, "Patty, what Paul decided to do is none of your business. Talk about what you did and how you felt. You can only change yourself; you are not responsible to change him." The unhealthy habit I had of trying to fix Paul with the unsound reasoning to "help him" was like a flashing neon light. Being made aware of dysfunctional behavior in a safe and caring environment, with people who kept me accountable to change, and a relationship with God to help me through, gradually began to transform me.

It turns out Linda was the woman I heard that first night, and she became my sponsor to help me one-on-one outside of group meetings. Linda was my age, and her birthday is the day before mine. I used to joke with her, "You're older than I am!" She was exactly the type of person I needed to bring out the best version of myself: no-nonsense or excuses; a sense of humor; commitment to meetings and doing the written work; availability when I needed her most; leadership at a higher level within Celebrate Recovery; teaching skills; and seeing the potential in me as a leader to take what I learned and help others.

Jeff Redmond, the Pastor of Recovery Ministries and leader of Celebrate Recovery, was a constant source of encouragement, humble authenticity, and who led by example. He challenged me to grow in my recovery journey and provided leadership training and roles within CR for me. Jeff and his wife, Debbie, generously gave caring support through many challenging times. He and Pastor Mark were the foundation of Biblical leadership that would counsel, pray for, and wisely direct Paul and me through our choices, responsibilities, and roles as Christian individuals and a married couple.

Over the next six years, I came out of denial and took responsibility for my attitude and behavior. I started to feel safe and shared secrets I had never told anyone before. The shame and condemnation I had carried for years was finally lifted off my shoulders. I stopped isolating myself and found I enjoyed being with women. We laughed, we prayed, and we cried. But most of all, we found healing.

My marriage started to change not because God was changing Paul, but because He was changing me. With the help of Celebrate Recovery and the counseling we continued to receive, both individually and as a couple, I learned how to stop engaging in conversations that turned critical. I wrote down my feelings in journals instead of telling Paul exactly what was on my mind. Writing down an argument allowed me to express myself without interruption or criticism, and I noticed patterns in behavior, especially mine. I shared my feelings and behavior with Linda or my step study group because I wanted to change. It was humbling, and change took longer than I thought. I still believed God could do a miracle in our marriage and change Paul as well as me. That hope kept me committed to the marriage.

One evening I was in my home office, with the door closed, while Paul watched TV. Working on my CR lesson answering the personal questions was often emotional as I had to honestly face my sinful and dysfunctional behavior and attitudes.

The door burst open, and I jerked my head up from my book, startled by Paul's unexpected presence. "What are you doing with the door closed?" Paul said brusquely.

"I'm doing my Step Study," I stuttered, catching my breath.

"I found your CR book hidden in your desk," he smirked.

"I told you it's private and to respect that!" I was angry and felt violated with his teasing and knowing he had probably read my intimate answers.

"We're not supposed to have secrets as a married couple. There must be a reason you're hiding it from me. The problem is you don't trust me," he said, trying to deflect the blame.

"You're right; I don't trust you! You quit your job and didn't tell me." I immediately regretted what I had said and thought *Help me, Lord.*

"I thought CR was helping you. Looks like you're reverting to your old self. You said you forgave me, and now you're bringing up the past again."

I paused and took a deep breath. "I'm sorry I criticized you. It was disrespectful. Please forgive me. I won't bring up the past again. Moving forward, please don't look in my private journals and CR Step Study books."

"Sure," he mumbled and walked away.

I've talked to a lot of women who struggle with the forgiveness passage in the Bible. For example, a husband does something hurtful, but says, "I'm sorry," and she forgives him. Then he does it again and again. This is how abuse continues.

The Bible says in Matthew 18:21-22, "Then Peter asked Jesus, 'Lord, how many times shall I forgive my brother or sister who sins against me? Up to seven times?'" Jesus answered, "I tell you, not seven times, but seventy-seven times." The Christian principle of *forgiveness* is to forgive others when they sin against us, just as God has forgiven us for our sins. Jesus is not saying to forgive over and over when a person continues to hurt you emotionally or physically.

Scripture is not a weapon for sinful, harmful behavior or to justify forgiveness. Paul combined forgiveness with the action to *forget* and said, "The Bible commands you to forgive. If you truly forgive me, you need to forget the past and stop bringing it up." *Forgive and forget* was used to manipulate me to believe his behavior would change if I always forgave him and forgot about his harmful behavior.

In Celebrate Recovery, I learned how to take responsibility for my words and actions instead of blaming others by letting go of control and asking forgiveness for my behavior. For the first time, I shared my secrets. I felt insecure being so vulnerable, and tears streamed down my flushed cheeks. I never knew, until then, that honesty and authenticity released the heavy guilt and shame I carried for years. I slept better at night and the migraines stopped. As the inside of me began to heal, I had a real smile that wasn't hidden under a mask. There was more time to enjoy life, as I found freedom from my people-pleasing habits.

The healthy behavior I learned gave me confidence and the strength to set boundaries and stand up for myself. The turning point in stopping abuse happened one afternoon when Paul came towards me with his clenched fist, ready to hit me for disagreeing with him about a money decision. I stood up tall, raised my hand in the air, looked him straight in the eye, and said, "If you hit me, I *will* call the police."

"You wouldn't dare call the police," he scowled. "You would be too embarrassed."

"No, you would be embarrassed when your name is in the newspaper tomorrow under police reports."

Paul glared at me, then whispered an abusive name under his breath. Then, he turned and left the room, and never hit me again. Change happened when I knew exactly what I wanted, clearly communicated it, and stood my ground.

I stayed in Celebrate Recovery for six years, became a leader, and was a sponsor for other women. I was in four Step Study groups as God peeled back the layers like an onion, revealing new issues I needed to work on, helping me break the bondage of my emotional eating, and find deeper healing.

Five ladies from one of my Step Studies joined me to start a morning recovery group called Life's Healing Choices, sponsored by Bayside Women's Ministry. It included free childcare for women with children so these hurting mothers could get help. Two of the ladies started a separate group specifically for domestic violence, became dear friends, and helped me to further understand my abuse. God continued to show me that I was not alone, and He had a purpose in my pain to help other women with theirs.

Occasionally, Paul Jr. would lead worship during CR. As a little boy, I remember him saying, "Mommy, I want to ask Jesus into my heart." Seeing him lead brought tears to my eyes. Here he was extending that same opportunity for a personal relationship to the men and women at CR who were broken, addicted, and abused.

Paul Jr. was now in his twenties, attended a local college, played guitar on the church worship team, and dated Kelly, who he met on a church mission trip. He and Kelly married in November 2013. I worried that our marriage problems negatively affected him. What I found was Paul Jr. was a good husband, cherished Kelly, and they enjoyed each other. They also proved to be financially responsible. Most importantly, they both had a solid relationship with God.

My mother prayed every day for her children and grandchildren. I watched over the years how she showed her love to each grandchild. Mother was a wonderful example of how a grandmother's relationship with her grandchildren should be. When she passed away, I found boxes of cards, notes, and drawings she had kept, many from her grandchildren. Reading what Mother's grandchildren said about her gave me a deeper insight into the loving relationships she had with them. This made me long for that type of relationship. So, I prayed for what I wanted next—grandchildren! My hope is that my granddaughters will feel the same love from me.

MONEY CAN'T BUY A RELATIONSHIP

In February 2014, my ninety-eight-year-old mother suddenly got ill from a leg infection. Her sharp mind quickly declined. She needed frequent care and moved into our home. I hired a live-in caregiver, Fina, to help with 24-hour care that included lifting, dressing, personal hygiene, light house cleaning and cooking, and keeping my mother company while I worked in my home office. Mother sat in her wheelchair for hours, peacefully staring out the window, or enjoying the flowers in my backyard. Sometimes I would give her a kiss and say, "What are you thinking about?"

She would smile and say, "I'm praying," or "Dad," or "How nice it is to be here."

Her simple life helped me to get a better perspective on my own. Yes, work is important, and there are responsibilities to take care of. But when I make relationships a priority and keep what needs to be done in proper focus, life is filled with purpose and very fulfilling.

When Fina had her days off, sometimes at night, I would hear Mother cry out, and I would run to her room, turn on the light, and gently stroke her hair. I would sing

Jesus Loves Me until she fell asleep. Then, I would whisper, "I love you, Mom," kiss her on the forehead, lovingly watch her sleep, and then slip quietly out of her room. It warmed my heart to have her with me every day.

On a Sunday, three weeks after she moved in, my brother, Peter, his wife, Margaret, and Mother's best friend, Jean, came for a visit. My brother brought communion for her.

The home care nurse who regularly checked on Mother's leg infection and happened to go to Bayside Church, called to see if she could come a day early. I said, "Of course! Some of my family is here."

When she arrived, Mother's vitals were checked. "I'm not getting normal oxygen readings. I need to call her doctor," she said anxiously. Within two minutes, the doctor instructed us to call an ambulance. I gave the medics Mother's health care directive and list of medications, and she was rushed to the hospital just across the street from our home.

My mind was in emergency mode, answering questions from the medical staff while trying to focus my thoughts on what was happening to my mother. My heart was pounding, and after what seemed like a long time, but was only a few minutes, the doctor came out and said, "Your mother is dying. We will keep her comfortable." I turned to my brother, who was standing next to me, and burst into tears. I wanted my mother to be with me so I could take care of her, like she had taken care of me. There was so much I wanted to talk to her about. I thought, *Why God? Why now?* But I didn't hear an answer.

I immediately called Paul Jr., and he and Kelly raced over. My son wrapped his arms around me, as I cried uncontrollably. My brother, Bill, and his wife, Kathy, arrived. Mother's friend, Jean, held him as tears flowed down his face. One of my best friends, Lisa, her husband, Vance, and their son, Ean, came right away. Lisa's warm embrace helped me to feel secure that I was not alone. Paul called Bayside's Care Pastor Mark, who had visited Mother a few days earlier when she was unusually restless and upset she couldn't find something. He soon arrived, and comforted Mother again with his words and prayers, and was the spiritual support I needed. Pastor Ray's wife, Carol, walked in and immediately hugged and prayed for me as I held back tears. My brother, Richard, and his wife, Amanda, weren't able to drive up.

I was trying to figure out how to process the news that my mother was dying when my phone rang. "Hi Patty, this is Ray. I'm sorry I can't be there. I would love to talk to your mother. Can you put me on speaker phone?" Without saying a word, I held the phone near Mom's ear. "Hi, Clare, this is Ray Johnston. You'll soon be in Heaven with Jesus. When you get there, please say hello to my mother and tell her I love her." Mom smiled. I felt a sense of peace and calmness come over me.

People handle death and grief differently, and for the next few hours, we each had time with Mother. She was in and out of consciousness. Some prayed and held Mom's hand. While some didn't say a word, others talked to her even though she didn't speak. Paul Jr. and I sang *Amazing Grace* and *Jesus Loves Me,* songs we know she loved listening to. Mother pointed to her ear, letting me know one of the hearing aids wasn't working. When I put in a new battery, a five-note melody played, and Mom smiled. She wanted to hear us.

Later that night, Mother was taken to a private room. Bill, Kathy, and I stayed vigilant by Mother's side. She was on heavy pain medication with her eyes closed. At midnight, expecting to spend many more hours with Mother, I left Bill and Kathy with her, tearfully got in my car, and drove home across the street to get some food for us.

Fina was sitting at the kitchen table. She looked up at me with worried eyes. I told her that Mother was dying. We both cried uncontrollably and held each other tight.

"Let's clean up Mother's room a little."

"That's a good idea," Fina whispered, as tears continued to roll down her cheeks. "I'll help you take the sheets and blanket off the bed. You will feel sad with Mama Clare gone."

When we finished tidying up the room, I started to pack food to take to the hospital. My phone rang! I hurried to answer it. It was Kathy. "Bill tried to call you, but no one answered. The nurse said your mother will be gone any minute."

I felt a sense of panic! I ran and jumped in the car, drove through stop signs, parked my car, and ran into the hospital. Kathy was waiting for me, and with tears in her eyes, she said, "Bill's in with Clare. She peacefully passed away two minutes ago."

I opened the door to my mother's room. Bill was sitting by her bed, crying. When he saw me, he didn't want to talk. I tried to understand his way of grieving, and put my hand on his shoulder. He walked silently out of the room, leaving me alone.

The nurse entered the room quietly and with reassuring words said, "You can stay as long as you want."

So, for the next hour, I cried, and held Mother's hand. It was cold to the touch, but I didn't let go. "I'm sorry I wasn't here, but I'm glad Bill was with you." I couldn't stop the tears from flowing. "Mother, I'm so upset I was doing work instead of being with you. I wanted to be with you in your last moments. I spend so much time working. I'm going to quit my proofreading business!"

As I held Mother's hand, I closed my eyes and was quiet. Then in her loving voice, I heard these words in my mind, "Patricia, you did so much for me. You're so good at your proofreading, and Patricia Fripp loves working with you. I want you to promise me that you will continue your business. I love you."

"Okay, Mom, I promise. Will you do something for me? I don't know if this is possible, but will you, from time to time, let me know you're with me? Give me a special sign that I know it's you." I didn't hear a response and stayed a few more minutes holding her hand. The nurse came in and said, "Whenever you're ready, there's a bag of your mother's personal belongings on the chair." I picked it up. There were her clothes and a small clear bag. As I reached to open it, I heard a familiar five-tone melody. My heart raced, and I looked at Mom as I wiped away my tears. "Thank you for being here. I love you. Say hi to Dad for me."

That would be the first of many times to this very day I have felt Mother's distinct presence. I don't know exactly what happens when we die, but I do know I miss her beyond words. I learned a hard lesson that night about the cost of putting work ahead of our relationships. For weeks I carried a burden of guilt. "If I hadn't made the choice to work, I would have been back with Mother in time."

I had sleepless and tearful nights as I played reruns in my head about the night my mother passed. My breakthrough came when I believed that God wanted my brother, Bill, to be with our mother in her last moments. I had a lot more time alone with her over the years than he did. The realization that we have choices in how we spend our time and can never get the time back changed my mindset about work. I made a conscious decision to prioritize relationships, and I continue to focus on that as I find myself battling with deadlines.

After my last night alone with my mother, the next four months were one of the most emotionally difficult times in my life. I have tears and heartache remembering it as I write. Mother's funeral was a tribute to her faith, family, and friends. The beautiful church in Tiburon was filled with people, and the view brought some of us a bit of happiness with the bright blue sky and sun shining down on the glistening water and Golden Gate Bridge. It was Mother's favorite view for fifty-five years.

After the funeral, life with the family got weird. It's interesting how family members show their selfishness about material items and money and mistrust for each other when parents pass away. I found out from many friends that it's very common, and we were no different. I had some of Mother and Dad's special possessions she wanted to bring to my home. My brother Peter and I were co-executors for Mother's living trust that included selling her expensive Tiburon home and dividing bank accounts. There was all the furniture, antiques, and possessions from sixty-five years of marriage. Some of the financial dealings with my three brothers were fine and even brought us closer together at times, but most of it was a time-consuming and emotional nightmare. If you've ever experienced the financial responsibility when a family member passes away, especially if there's significant money involved, you know exactly what I'm talking about.

With my inheritance money, I wanted to open an account in my name only. One afternoon, while we were relaxing by the pool, I said to Paul, "I've been thinking about my inheritance and wanted you to know, I'm going to the bank today to open an account."

"It's a lot of money. Why don't we go together and then out to dinner to celebrate." He reached over, stroked my leg, and smiled.

"We could do that," I agreed, standing up from the lounge chair. "But, I'm going to put the account in my name only."

He stared at me, his smile turning to a frown. "The Bible says we are one as a married couple. Your mother's inheritance is <u>our</u> money. My name should be on the bank account. Don't you trust me?"

I thought, *Wow, here he goes again using the Bible. Do I trust him? No. We've argued about money ever since we got married.* I took a deep breath. "I've already talked to a few people at church about my decision. There were mixed feelings. Two women said their husbands agreed with them that the money they make is their money. Two other women combine everything with their husbands. They all said to pray about it and do what I think is best and don't be selfish and keep it for myself."

"So, did you pray about it?"

I stared at him and said, "Of course."

"You don't trust God," Paul grumbled.

"What?" I exclaimed in a loud voice.

Paul glared at me, "If you did, you wouldn't be selfish with the money."

"I trust God, but I don't trust you!" I yelled!

"I knew it! You've never accepted me."

"You're irresponsible! How soon will it be until you lose this job?" I scowled.

"Always bringing up the past. You never encourage me!" Paul lashed back.

I knew where this was headed, and I had engaged in the "dance" Paul and I had done for years with blaming, attacking character, name-calling, and shouting judgmental "You" statements at each other.

"I'm walking away from this. I'm angry and feeling frustrated. We can talk later." Paul murmured something as I walked into the house. I ignored it, changed out of my bathing suit, got in my car, and drove to the bank. I felt empowered with that much money and secure that, with me controlling the account, we would never be in debt again. If

I wanted to play golf or spend money on something special, I didn't have to ask permission or get criticized for overspending. A smile beamed across my face as I daydreamed about what I could do with the money.

When I got back home, I apologized for what I said and shared two ideas I had for part of my inheritance. One was to pay down our mortgage faster and the other to travel with Bayside Church to the Holy Land.

"That sounds great!" Paul grinned as his eyes lit up.

I immediately paid off our debt to my brother, Richard, and put money in our joint savings. The terrible mistake I made with my inheritance was to make several financial decisions without wise counsel and planning for the future. I also kept believing, despite many red flags, that our marriage would get better. I bought into a timeshare and put it in both of our names, which I would later have to fight for in the divorce settlement. We added an expensive patio cover for our backyard, some home furnishings, and I paid for a few nice vacations.

A beautiful new gym had opened next to our neighborhood, and I told Paul, "This will be a fun and healthy way to be together." Paul Jr. and Kelly joined, and many of our neighbors and friends from church. I started to feel better about myself, was exercising almost every day, and eating healthier. I had hope for our marriage and the future.

Our trip to the Holy Land was the best decision I made. It allowed wonderful friendships and memories to be created, including with a couple who would become dear friends of mine—John and Laura Volinski. They would play an important part in my transition to a new season in life. The trip was a bonding time for our marriage. Paul publicly apologized to me, in front of the group, for his abusive behavior. With his promise to end it, I suddenly saw him in a better light and was extremely attracted to him. I found renewed belief that God was changing both of us.

When we got home, I was less critical by not accusing Paul of being lazy or bringing up past job losses. I was more encouraging by praising his skills and years of experience that contributed to his success. I took better responsibility for my actions, and worked hard to let others—especially Paul—be responsible for themselves, and tried not to control them with the motivation to "help them." The next two years were less volatile for our marriage. We both worked, volunteered at church, were leaders in a married couples group, and worked out together at the new gym.

As a leader in Celebrate Recovery, I took changing myself very seriously. I knew others would look at me as a role model as I did with my sponsor, Linda. Dealing with my own issues in a safe and caring environment—where I got accountability for my unhealthy behavior—was key to the transformation God was making in my life. I began to understand my mother's words, "Patricia, you need to take care of yourself."

Those of you in an abusive relationship will hopefully learn from my mistakes, especially the financial ones. If you end up divorced or your partner leaves you, the financial challenges you face can be overwhelming. Don't assume the other person will be thoughtful and fair. I know of divorces that have financially worked out agreeably, but many have not. Women sadly stay in an abusive relationship out of financial fear they can't make it alone.

I guarantee money does not change an abusive relationship. It may help with paying the bills and in other financial areas, but change only happens when a person makes the choice to change themselves with God's help. My involvement in Celebrate Recovery, Life's Healing Choices, and all Bayside Church services and events would soon come to an abrupt stop.

MY HUMILIATING TURNING POINT

When you were a child, did you ever have a nightmare? How did you feel when you woke up? Frightened of the dark? Hysterical? Was someone there to comfort you and help you go back to sleep? I had nightmares as a child and teenager. My mother was always there to turn on the light, put her loving arms around me, and say, "Patricia, I'm here. It was only a dream." Sometimes she sang *Jesus Loves Me*, and I always felt better. But one time, Mother wasn't there to comfort me after the most traumatic nightmare of my life.

In April 2016, I sat on the couch talking to Paul. "Last weekend was frightful, but I want you to know I forgive you. After thirty years of marriage, we will get through this together." Suddenly, there was a loud banging on the front door. I walked over to peer out the blinds. I recognized the guy from the local TV news. I opened the door just enough to put my head out.

The reporter thrust a microphone in my face. "Can I ask you a few questions?" A cameraman stood at the end of the walkway. Sadly, I knew why the reporter was there. I shook my head no, stepped back, closed the door, and locked it. I frantically ran around to close all the blinds. I fought back tears and thought, *What the hell just happened? How did I get here?*

Just a few weeks prior, Paul and I were sitting on the couch after church talking about something that happened at the gym.

"Remember a detective came by and talked to you three weeks ago when I was at work?"

"Yes, he told me there was an incident at the gym and for you to call him."

"Well, I talked to him twice."

"Why didn't you tell me sooner?"

"I was afraid you would divorce me. I need to confess, but you must promise not to tell anyone," he said with tears in his eyes. Paul began to reveal his dark secret. When he was done, he begged for forgiveness.

I had mixed emotions, but I tearfully said, "I forgive you. We will get through this together. You need to tell Paul Jr. This is too serious for him not to know."

Paul stared at me and finally answered, "I will. The lawyer said we can't tell anyone, even your family."

"Okay, I just want you to tell our son. We need to pray now."

Paul reached out his hands. I hesitated but then took his trembling hands in mine. We prayed. Afterward, I looked directly into his eyes and said, "We've been married almost thirty years. Unless God makes it clear to me otherwise, I'll stay with you, and we'll get through this together." I let go of his hands that were still shaking.

"Thank you. God will get us through. I'm not a criminal, Patty."

Later that day, I went to the gym and canceled his membership.

That afternoon, I had to prepare for an upcoming photo shoot for a local magazine. Paul and I, together with Paul Jr. and Kelly would be the featured community family on the cover with an article in April's edition. I was nervous and tears ran down my cheeks as I struggled with the hypocrisy of it all. I couldn't talk to anyone about this and didn't know what to do.

For the next two weeks, I endured intense, emotional turmoil. I experienced countless feelings, including fear, betrayal, anger, resentment, anxiety, hypocrisy, and confusion. My promise to Paul not to tell anyone was a horrible mistake. The deception to keep his secret from everyone, including not telling my son, sacrificed my emotional freedom as I protected the man I once believed was Prince Charming. I put on a cheerful mask of secrecy, but headaches and nausea plagued my body.

I asked Paul a couple of times, "Have you told Paul Jr. yet?"

His reply was always, "I will."

I prayed for direction on what to do, but God seemed to be silent. I thought, *He can do the impossible. The Bible says God works all things together for His good. I need to wait and trust Him.*

Whenever I saw Paul Jr., Kelly, and our church friends, I acted like everything was okay. But inside I felt depressed. I was a hypocrite. But of course, I had learned to be an expert at keeping secrets.

One Friday, Paul called me from work. "I just got a call from my lawyer. The police are on their way to arrest me.

I'll be in jail overnight. You need to pick up my car," he said with no emotion in his voice.

"Oh my God, arrest you?" my voice trembled as I spoke.

"Patty, I can't talk anymore. Just pick up my car. Don't tell anybody. I'll call you from jail."

Early the next morning, I went to the jail and picked Paul up. He was tense and didn't want to talk much. That afternoon we met with Paul Jr. and Kelly to look at photos of the recent photoshoot. They were excited and happy. I pretended to be just as excited. But deep down inside, I wanted to tell them so badly everything that had happened, but Paul didn't say anything. So, I knew I couldn't either. Once again, I felt isolated and alone in prison.

Three days later, I turned on the news and was devastated to see Paul's photo and hear the reporter say, "This man was arrested Friday on suspicion of molesting someone. Police believe there may be other victims out there. We tried to interview an unidentified woman who wouldn't speak to us." I was stunned and looked in horror as I saw myself on TV peering out our front door.

I frantically called Paul at work. "Your arrest is on the news!"

"The news is getting around the department, too." Paul sounded agitated. "My boss wants me to leave right away for my safety."

"I'm going over to tell Paul and Kelly what I know."

"Don't tell them everything! The lawyer said we're not supposed to talk to anyone," Paul said forcefully.

"I don't care what the lawyer said. This is my son. You said you would tell him and never did. I'm going over now."

He quickly said, "Can't you wait until I get home? We need to do this together."

I felt manipulated by his "we need" words that were too late. "No, I'm going by myself. I'll talk to you when you get home."

As I drove to their apartment, I was breathing hard, and my hands were shaking from the shock of the darkest secret being suddenly exposed to what felt like the world. I prayed, "Lord, please give me wisdom on what to say, and what not to. I'm angry at Paul for putting Paul Jr, Kelly, and me through this. I'm not going to cover up for him anymore! Show me what to do."

When my son opened the door, my eyes filled with tears when I saw the serious look on his face. I took a deep breath and didn't let myself cry because the time was about them, not my emotions. My legs felt weak as I slowly sat down on a chair across from Kelly. She was quiet, and Paul sat next to her.

With a stern look in his eyes, he said, "Mom, we want to know exactly what happened with Dad. Don't hold anything back from us. We've been getting calls and text messages from people who saw it on the news. Kelly and I are upset and afraid the police or someone might show up at our door. I have the same name as Dad."

My heart ached for them as I replied, "I'll tell you everything I know and am so sorry you had to find out this way. I told Dad many times he needed to let you know." I went on to share everything I knew, even what Paul and the lawyer wanted confidential. I wasn't there to protect my husband, but to build a relationship with my son and his wife. They asked questions, including if I was going to divorce Paul. My voice trembled as I slowly replied, "God hasn't released me from the marriage, so I'm staying to support him. I'll see what happens."

When I got up to leave, Paul Jr. hugged me and said, "Thanks for telling us everything. I'll call you so we can get together again later today." Kelly and I held onto each other a little longer, aware of the emotional stress of this crisis.

That would be the last time I saw them for six months. My decision to stay with Paul would cost me a painful separation from my son that I had never experienced before. The severe impact of Paul's choices would reach farther than he realized or would ever apologize and take responsibility for.

I went into complete isolation. My dream home became a prison. I kept the shades pulled and only went out late at night for groceries. Phone calls, text messages, and private Facebook comments overwhelmed me.

Some friends and family didn't know what to say and were silent, while others wouldn't acknowledge me when I said hello. At first, their reactions felt hurtful. I was encouraged when some friends said, "It's not your fault. Are you okay? How is Paul Jr.? What can I do to help you? Can I take you to coffee or lunch?" The most surprising response was, "Let me tell you about the time my name was in the news."

Paul lost his job and income. So, I used my inheritance to pay for his lawyer and expenses when our savings was gone. The financial pressure increased. His legal case lasted a year. The uncertainty of a court decision and sentence pulled me closer to God. I fell on my knees in prayer, tears streaming down my face, asking, *How did I get to this awful place in my life?* I longed to know God's purpose for me in all this chaos.

God waited for me to take off the mask of secrecy to reveal my true self and move me toward His purpose. I decided to expose my years of lies, sinful behavior, and secrets to my counselor and a few close friends. I discovered an inner strength and a new perspective on who I was and the life I wanted. The change He wanted to make would manifest itself through His plan.

Paul was convicted of a misdemeanor charge of indecent exposure. The sentence included three months in jail, three years on probation, and a lifetime registration as a sex offender.

My time alone for three months was an unfamiliar experience. The peace and freedom from daily tension and conflict was a significant blessing. There were fewer tears and more smiles on my face, and joy in my heart. I listened to Christian music and danced and sang around the house. I laughed with friends and enjoyed relaxing walks. Now, I understand why I don't deserve to be abused by anyone, yet I continued to hope for a better marriage.

When Paul came home from jail, my peace and freedom left. I felt imprisoned again because conflict and emotional and verbal abuse quickly returned. He called me insulting names, minimized my feelings, mocked what I said, and shamed me for trying to change. The mental abuse made me question my sanity, perception of reality, and memory.

Every month, the police pounded on our door, walked through the house, and interrogated us. My heart raced during the whole ordeal. I held back tears and felt punished and violated for something that wasn't my fault. I questioned God about my future. "Lord, my dream has become a nightmare! Do You want me to share Paul's consequences for the rest of my life? I'm exhausted and confused, and I don't know if You want me to stay or leave." I trusted God would answer, but I had to wait on Him.

God provided me with a new dream. Paul Jr. and Kelly invited me to lunch and gave me a toy guitar with a sign that read, "Future rock star joining the band in 2018." I jumped up and down with excitement, and tears of joy filled my eyes! The thought of finally being a grandmother warmed my heart, brought visions of holding a sweet baby in my arms, and made me think about my legacy.

DO I STAY OR LEAVE?

Despite years of counseling, Paul promising to do better, and even with the trauma I had been put through after his arrest, the emotional and verbal assaults continued. Our thirtieth wedding anniversary was hard for me. I was having serious doubts there would be a thirty-first, but God hadn't made it clear to me that I was free to leave Paul.

In November 2017, Paul encouraged me to attend a women's retreat, saying, "It would endear me to you even more." It was called, "He Heals the Brokenhearted," by Kairos Outside. This Christian-based retreat's purpose was to demonstrate God's grace and love to women personally affected by someone that went to jail or prison.

I received a letter from Paul during the retreat. He thought the experience would help me "Understand and empathize" with his experience of incarceration, reinforce that "God is a God of restoration and reconciliation," and "Put the past behind us as we press on together to see what He has in store for us." Psalm 147:3 in the Bible says, "He heals the brokenhearted and binds up their wounds." What I came away with was continual reinforcement by the leaders and women I met that I did not deserve to be abused and needed Paul to stop or leave him. This Biblical truth finally got through to me after years of false hope, secrets, and toleration.

When I got home, Paul and I met with two of our pastors. We discussed the *Boundaries and Consequences of Verbal Abuse* I put together. As a result of counsel, prayer, reflection, and my retreat, I had reached a point of zero tolerance for what I considered abuse. If Paul continued his actions, he would move out. The pastors were supportive of my decision, counseled us on what changes we each needed to make, and prayed for God's direction and presence in our lives.

Three months later, after counseling and trying hard to make our marriage work, we were back meeting with the pastors. We discussed the *Terms of Separation* that he and I agreed to. Paul planned to use the separation time to be with his family and friends in southern California because his mother had just passed away.

When Paul left, I was alone again, and my carefree dancing and positive spirit returned. My dear friend, Denise, and counselor, Lisa, both said, "You are a different person without Paul. God doesn't expect you to stay in an abusive relationship. Do you want to live that way the rest of your life?"

"No, I don't want to be abused ever again, but I don't believe God has released me from the marriage yet." I thought about what they said and prayed every day that God would show me what to do. I also fervently prayed for my grandchild that would be born the next month, what type of relationship we would have, and the Christian legacy I wanted to leave for Paul Jr., my grandchildren, and into the future.

One morning, as I read my Bible and prayed, God spoke to me through my thoughts. I heard His quiet voice distinctly say, "I have plans for you that are greater than your life now. You have faithfully waited on Me. I release you from your marriage." My body was tingling, and I had goosebumps on my arms. There was no doubt I had heard from God. I felt total peace as my body relaxed, and I took a few deep breaths. I began to cry for the loss of my childhood dream, and experienced a newly found joy as I embraced the hope of an exciting new one. I closed my eyes as I thanked God for His answer and thought about the blessing of a better life.

With God's green light of release, I was adamant I would not live with any more abuse. Fed up with someone who pulled me down when I sought God's best, I boldly moved forward with a divorce. I got advice from my counselor, talked to a few people I respected and trusted, and wrote the steps I needed to take. I hired an excellent attorney, Carsen Tazi, and felt confident in her and the journey ahead. I changed the locks on the doors, got security cameras, and felt safe.

I called Paul and told him about the divorce. He was angry and started to criticize me.

"Goodbye, Paul," I said calmly and hung up the phone. I felt good about how I handled myself and the decision.

On March 24th, Kelly's mother, Debbie, and I were anxiously waiting at the hospital for the announcement. I still remember our tearful and excited reaction when Paul Jr. came out and proudly said, with a smile that glowed across his face, "It's a girl!" Debbie and I jumped up and down, hugging each other while tears of joy streamed down our faces. We lovingly embraced the excited new father, and were beside ourselves with excitement to see and hold our first grandchild.

Addison was beautiful, with curls in her hair like Kelly. My heart melted as her tiny fingers held onto mine, and her huge smile and deep blue eyes shined up at me. Every chance

I got, I cuddled and kissed her, sang *Jesus Loves Me,* and prayed for the life and purpose God would have for this priceless child. Being a grandmother became my greatest joy in life.

I hope you are encouraged by my story and know that there is help for you to escape the imprisonment of abuse. We each have our own unique journey, and the choice is ours to take the first courageous step down a different path that leads to freedom.

THE TRANSITION

Have you ever downsized from a home to an apartment? What was your greatest challenge? For me, it was decluttering sixty years of my life! I am a recovering "paperholic!" I kept more than the IRS requires of seven years of tax returns. If money had been spent, I likely had the receipt. If you wanted maps of Disneyland dating back years, I had them. I kept travel brochures of places we had vacationed—you can imagine the folders in filing cabinets, of which there were at least six. With several businesses over the years, I was prepared for any audit...which <u>never</u> came. I had almost every school paper, drawing, and report card for Paul Jr. My love for photos is a blessing and curse—like some of you, my largest phone storage is digital photos!

The transition to my new life took two moves, a trip across the country, several shows of organization expert, Marie Kondo, and *The Minimalist* online series, and thousands of hours and trips to recycling. For three months, I did all the preparation and packing with the support of family, friends, and neighbors. During my emotional, physical, and financial divorce challenges, God provided caring and generous people to be there for me.

One day, Paul came to the house and scared me when he tried to unlock the door and peered in the front window. I quickly hid in the hallway so he couldn't see me. When his key didn't work, he pounded on the door. My heart was racing as I pretended not to be home. Our written agreement was he would call first. After that, I always kept the doors and yard gates locked. Although he adamantly denied ever being there, security cameras don't lie.

I never allowed Paul to enter the house until we met with our realtor to discuss the sale of the house. When the realtor left, Paul continuously criticized me for not letting him look around the house. He didn't know I had arranged for my neighbor, John, to come over if I needed him. When I started to call John, Paul quickly went out the front door, slamming it behind him.

I suggest if you are in an abusive relationship and live separately, that you take safety precautions like changing the locks and installing video cameras. It's an inexpensive way to invest in your self-care and protection and will help you feel safer and sleep better at night.

Our house was no longer my dream home. As soon as it went on the market, it immediately sold for full price. I was in awe of how quickly God worked this part of His plan.

I was content and happy to live in an apartment just down the street from Paul Jr., Kelly, and my beautiful granddaughter, Addie. There would soon be another major change for me, but God allowed me time to learn how to take care of myself.

Part 4

IS THAT REALLY ME IN THE MIRROR?

When I finally made the choice to leave my marriage, there were a lot of decisions I needed to make. Some were personal choices, others the result of my ex-husband's behavior, and there were decisions I had no control over. The common thread in all of them, especially in hindsight, is that God was with me the entire time, even when I didn't think He was there.

When I look back at who I saw in the mirror when the physical abuse first began, I feel ashamed of my hidden and distorted image. My self-esteem was low, I was a people pleaser, and my desire to help others often led to controlling behavior. I had limited knowledge of what it takes from two people to create a healthy marriage, especially how to handle conflict, take personal responsibility, and work together as a supportive couple.

This section will reveal the new, authentic, and transformed image I found in the mirror. We all have choices of how we view our reflection in a mirror, and it often involves changing ourselves. I have met hundreds of women who have made the change from abuse to freedom, and it all began when we made the choice to do something about it. The stories of victory continue to bring joy to my heart and tears to my eyes.

THE IMPORTANCE OF SELF-CARE

Do you remember any advice your mother gave you? Two key points that I recall are, "If you can't say anything nice, don't say anything at all," and "Patricia, you need to take care of yourself." I'm pretty sure the first one was because I had a tendency to talk back to my parents and had my mouth washed out with soap—but only once! The second was because I was a people pleaser, and frequently took care of other people's needs before my own.

My third-grade teacher wrote on my report card, "Patricia is a superior student in all things and is much admired by the whole class. She is quite restless. She should try to lose herself in a good story. Instead, she wanders about straightening the room, which is nice, but I would be happy to see her enjoying a book." When I read this a few years ago, I cried for the little girl who wanted to clean instead of relax and read. Even at that young age, not only was my perfectionism beginning to show, but self-care was not something I knew how to do.

After Mother passed away, I was going through cards and notes she had given me over the years. I paused to read a note dated February 7, 2011. "Dear Patricia, It's such a beautiful day. I want you to go for a nice walk. It's time you take care of yourself instead of everyone else. I love you very much, and I know you are going to do okay with your new change! Walk, walk, walk! Love, Mother." I burst into tears.

At the time, I had gained about fifty pounds since being married. The only self-care I did was an occasional manicure. I had just spent a few days with my mother before starting a new job as an usher for the River Cats, a Sacramento baseball team. I remember during the job interview, the guy looked at me and said, "There's a lot of walking up and down stairs. Do you think you will have any problems?"

I looked him straight in the eye. "Young man, I've been here five hours and stood in lines the entire time. You are my fourth interview. If I can do that, I can certainly walk up and down stairs!"

"You're hired!" he announced.

I take after my mother when it comes to self-care. She probably realized what the lack of self-care had cost her over sixty-five years of marriage, but her words of advice over the years just weren't getting through to me until I found her note in December 2018.

The timing was significant. I was decluttering stacks of boxes from my recent move from a large four-bedroom house to a small two-bedroom apartment. I was in the middle of a divorce and having a difficult time with my identity, financial situation, and what my future looked like.

Two months before, I was invited by a friend to High-Performance Expert, Brendon Burchard's Academy, to learn skills and best practices to become an expert in my business. I was depressed and told my friend, Nok, "I don't know who Brendon is, but I'll go with you just to get away for a few days." I had very low expectations, and relaxing was at the top of my list.

Little did I know that God had a plan for me to meet two women who would become dear friends, among my biggest cheerleaders, and influence the direction of my life. One was Dr. Erin Oksol, who wrote the Foreword of this book. She saw the potential in me to become a confident and successful editor, and asked me to edit what would become her best-selling book *Mind Your Own Business*. The other person was Pamela Zimmer, a messenger from God saying, "Patty, I am an expert in this and will help you get started. *Self-care isn't selfish, it's essential.*"

For the next three months, Pamela coached me by phone, texts, voicemail, and email to learn simple, but powerful ways to take better care of myself. It didn't mean to ignore people I loved, but through self-care, I would be in a healthier place emotionally, physically, and spiritually to be available for them.

At first, I felt guilty focusing on myself, and it was hard writing down ideas like:

- What activities did I enjoy at home?
- What did my ideal workweek look like?
- How would I ideally spend my free time and with who?
- What energized and filled me up?
- What made me smile and laugh?
- What did I do for self-care?
- What did the BEST version of myself look like?

What I've found over time is, in addition to the wonderful manicures and massages, my self-care includes:

- Taking a walk
- Enjoying a nap

- Reading a book
- Having breakfast, lunch, dinner, or coffee with a friend
- Going to a movie with someone or alone
- Working out at the gym
- Swimming
- Taking care of my plants and flowers
- Going on a hike with a friend or by myself
- Putting on music and dancing
- Sitting in my favorite rocking chair and closing my eyes for a few minutes
- Being with my granddaughters
- Spending daily time in Bible reading and meditation with God.

I found that the key to my turning point from a struggling victim to a healthy survivor was the realization that I needed to take care of myself. I started to put aside some of the money that I earned from editing, birthday gifts, and other sources specifically for self-care. Mother was able to witness the early stages when I began to get manicures and pedicures.

Being raised with three brothers and having a son, I never understood why women spent so much money on their nails! My cousin, Pamela, who was a marketing director for a well-known nail product company, would send mother and me expensive polish, oils, foot scrubs, and lotions. When Paul Jr. started dating Kelly, she and I had a girls' date at the nail salon. Except for laughing hysterically when the bottoms of my feet were brushed, it was a luxurious experience, and I was hooked! The next time I visited Pamela, she showed me how to save money and do my own nails in between the occasional mani-pedi at the salon.

When I inherited money after Mother passed away, I began to schedule massages. Paul didn't like me spending the money, but when I scheduled a few couple massages, he stopped complaining. During the traumatic period after Paul was arrested, his year-long court case, and then when I filed for divorce, the relaxing and healing touch of a massage helped to get me through the physical and emotional pain I felt.

When I moved to North Carolina, I found a new form of self-care. My son started playing on the Elevation Worship team, and I met the gifted team leader Chandan. I would occasionally see his beautiful wife Laura and briefly say hello as she lovingly, with her distinct southern voice, navigated her very pregnant body and four children through the crowd to the children's area. We became friends on Facebook, and I began to find out there was an inspiring and phenomenal side to Laura that would change how I looked at myself at almost seventy.

Just like I minimized spending time on my nails, my skincare was simple—wash my face with water and whatever facewash seemed to feel good. I was fortunate to inherit young-looking skin like my mother. However, being in the sun a lot, unhealthy eating habits, and the advance of time was starting to catch my skin up with my age.

When I met Laura, she was one of the top leaders in the Rodan + Fields (R+F) skincare company. It's not about her incredibly successful position that made her stand out to me. What I noticed was her deep faith and family commitment, generous and caring heart, and sincere desire to help others. She sees the unique and priceless individual inside me and wants the outside to reflect the beauty within.

Over the last three years, I have had more compliments on my skin than ever, and many people think I'm fifteen to twenty years younger. If you compare my photos from a few years ago with those today, you can see the physical effect of abuse, stress, and trauma on me and what a difference self-care means.

When I look in the mirror now, the shame of my abuse has been replaced with pride in looking the best I can because I take care of myself. Thank you to Pamela and Laura, who I believe God has used to impact my physical, emotional, and spiritual life and help me fulfill obedience to my dear mother's advice, "Patricia, you need to take care of yourself."

If you want to know more about the importance of self-care and skincare, you can read Pamela's and Laura's valuable advice in the Resource section of this book.

A NEW START, DREAM, AND LEGACY

In early 2019, Paul Jr. came to me and said, "Kelly and I are thinking about moving to North Carolina."

"I'm going with you!" I replied immediately. My beautiful granddaughter Addison was a year old, and I didn't want distance to separate us. The embrace of her tiny body next to mine brought countless smiles to my face and kisses to hers.

We traveled to North Carolina in March to see if this was the right decision. Kelly had relatives here, home prices were a lot lower than in California, and Paul Jr. had been following Elevation Worship for a couple of years. Never in a million years had I thought about moving out of California, let alone 3,000 miles across the country to the South.

The moment I arrived, I knew this was home. People were amazingly friendly. There were churches and American flags wherever I looked, and anyone younger than I am called me *ma'am* and *Miss Patty*. There was politeness, respect, and Southern hospitality.

The first time I went to Elevation Church in Charlotte, I was greeted by a friendly young woman who introduced herself as Giovanna and said, "You can call me Gia." She noticed I had been dancing as she walked up and said, "Are you new here?"

"Yes." I assumed they weren't used to people dancing at church, which I would soon find out was incorrect.

"Where are you from, and what brings you to Elevation?"

"I'm from California, and I'm here with my son and his family. We're thinking about moving out here. I found an apartment I like near here."

"I live nearby at Bexley," Gia replied.

"Bexley! That's where the apartment is." Turns out, Gia's apartment was in the building next to the one I liked.

Gia inquired, "What areas of Charlotte have you seen so far?" I told her, and she asked, "Have you been to the Billy Graham Library yet?"

"It was on my list, but I just didn't have time. I'm flying home tomorrow."

Gia smiled, "You know it's right on the way to the airport, and I work there. I'm an assistant editor for *Decision Magazine*. You could stop for a tour and lunch."

"An editor! I'm an editor, but I help people write books."

Gia said, "Here's my number. Call me, and we'll meet. The service is about to start, and you don't want to miss Pastor Steven Furtick preach and Elevation Worship."

We hugged, and I ran into the service. The worship and preaching at Elevation were phenomenal, and I felt God saying, "Welcome home."

I had four months to declutter and pack, say goodbye to friends and family, and think about my new life in North Carolina. Five weeks before my trip, I was scheduled to volunteer, for the seventh time, at a celebrity golf tournament in Lake Tahoe. As I started to drive to this exciting event, I noticed the vision in my left eye was slightly blurred. I thought it might be from staying up late countless nights in a row getting ready to move. I put some eyedrops in, but that didn't help. There was no pain, and I wasn't worried because my eyes often felt dry from my editing work. I was sure my vision would clear up in a few minutes.

Almost ten minutes later, I was having trouble focusing on the road and the cars in front of me. I thought, *My eye doctor's office is right up this road. I'll stop and have him quickly look at it, and then be on my way to Tahoe.* As I sat in the exam chair, I chatted with Dr. Okomoto, a huge golf fan, about the tournament and my upcoming move to North Carolina. He suddenly stopped talking, and a serious look came on his face.

"Patty, you're not going to Tahoe. I'm sending you to the hospital. I don't know why, but your left retina has detached. You're lucky you didn't drive up to the mountains. The pressure would have caused you to lose your eyesight. I'm hoping a special laser treatment will repair it. You won't be able to drive for three weeks, and must wear a patch over your eye during that time. Don't lift anything over ten pounds, and sit and walk with your head tilted down. If it works, you'll be in North Carolina next month. If not, you'll be in bed, face down, for the next six to eight weeks."

I felt overwhelmed by this huge crisis, and fear engulfed my body. I tried not to think about the "what if" scenarios and possibly losing my eyesight. There was still a chance my eye would be permanently damaged. You can imagine my fear as I thought about my job as an editor, an important source of income, possibly ending. How could I finish my packing if I had to sit and not lift anything heavy? Who would drive me to doctor appointments and on errands?

When I got home, I cried uncontrollably. I thought, *Why God? Why now? Haven't I gone through enough?* He was silent, and I prayed and read my Bible more frequently and fervently than I ever had before. The laser treatment went well, and during the three weeks of recovery, God was with me, as He had been in all my crisis situations. He provided everything I needed.

I felt humbled and grateful that my generous and thoughtful son drove me everywhere, and the time together was a precious gift from God. Kelly and her mother gladly fixed meals for me. My friends came over, brought food, and helped pack. It was fun and truly memorable. Some items on my long to-do list didn't get done, and that was okay. I learned, once again, the importance of relationships over work. God taught me that He could be trusted in any situation and was always with me.

Three weeks later, the doctor took the patch off my eye. "*Pirate Patty*, it's okay for you to drive now." We laughed, and I hugged him, grateful for the years of care he provided for my precious eyesight.

My long-time friend, Cori, helped me make the epic and memorable trip across the country. We stopped at places like beautiful Sedona, the breathtaking Grand Canyon, and the capital of country music, Nashville! I am thankful to have shared that "bucket list" trip with her.

By August 2019, we had all moved to Charlotte, North Carolina. Kelly's parents would soon follow, and her sister and husband. The love of your grandchildren causes you to make crazy decisions that are priceless. I have no regrets about mine.

I quickly made friends, especially the apartment "Bexley Belles," as we called ourselves, many of whom were close to my age and grandparents. I immediately got involved at Elevation Church as a greeter with Gia, welcoming people from all over the world. I've since joined the Elevation Church choir, and sing and praise the Lord with one of the greatest worship teams in the world. God brought me to a beautiful, yet unfamiliar part of the country to show me the greater plans He had promised.

I was humbled and grateful as I saw God's best plan for me manifesting a new dream. I joined a group of savvy business women and was the only white woman. Although my skin color was different, I felt tremendous love and acceptance. Abuse is colorblind to race, age, and gender. I cried when I heard their stories of abuse.

My divorce was plagued by money disagreements, which caused the divorce settlement to drag on for two years. Again, God spoke to me, "The stress and time over money imprisons you. Let it go and move on. Trust Me." So, in March 2020, I settled the divorce. Finally, I savored the sweet taste of freedom. A week later, the world began to shut down due to Covid-19. I marveled at God's timing and was grateful I listened to Him. The long-term investment of trusting God's wisdom I found in the words of Jeremiah 29:11. "For I know the plans I have for you," declares the Lord, "plans to prosper you and not to harm you, plans to give you hope and a future."

The year 2020 was the cornerstone of God's greater journey for me. In July, I joined an award-winning publishing company as an editor, and now my business reaches people worldwide. The dynamic Christian publisher, Joan T. Randall, challenged me to write this book in July 2020, but I wasn't ready. I first wrote a short story about my abuse titled "Freedom from the Mask of Secrecy," which was published in an international best-selling book, *The Image in the Mirror II*. The anthology with fifteen other authors was made into a documentary.

I now have a best-selling e-book called *Simple Strategies to Structure Your Story*. I have plans to do more writing. After twenty-five years of thinking about it, I finally have a beautiful website designed by my creative friend, Nadia. Mother would be proud of me that I not only kept my promise to continue my proofreading business, but at seventy-two years old, have a digital business card!

God continues to reveal more of who He created me to be and has provided meaningful opportunities for me to grow. His promise of a better life for me included healthy and loving family relationships. In September 2020, joy radiated from my heart at the birth of my second granddaughter, Isabella. God's blessing is that I will leave a legacy for my granddaughters with a story that has a happy ending.

The theme song for my life should be "Overcomer," by Mandisa. I don't quit or give in. I hold on tight to God, knowing there's nothing impossible with Him. And when I have my moments of feeling down or hopeless, God reminds me that I'm an overcomer. Hopefully, by reading this book, you've found encouragement, motivation, and practical advice to help you overcome whatever trials or trauma you experience.

I hope and pray that you find freedom from abuse as I did. It starts with a choice to change and get help. The Bible says in Matthew 19:26, "With man this is impossible, but with God all things are possible."

The journey out of the *prison of secrecy* can be very difficult, but not impossible. The key to unlock the door is available to anyone who takes the first step. For me, it was the choice to change. The healing process of taking off my mask of secrecy includes another powerful breakthrough. I'm proud to say I've lost twenty pounds! I can feel Mother's arms hugging me tightly and hear her loving voice say, "Patricia, you've learned to take care of yourself."

So, even if you're afraid like I was, you can take off the mask, and with God's help, you can change, and discover a purpose-filled life!

BECOMING A MAN OF PURPOSE THROUGH FAMILY CRISIS

*"I didn't experience any abuse growing up, but I do have a
story to tell."*

By Paul Lauterjung, Jr.

"The year 2016 was one for the record books because there
were so many things happening at the same time—my
father was arrested and the story was blasted over the local
news; family members checked into various rehabilitation
centers; stress brought the onset of panic attacks; being told
"No" for the church job I really wanted; and almost being
fired from my full-time job. Hindsight really is 20/20
because looking back now, I wouldn't change a single thing
that happened. There's a saying, *Rough seas make stronger
sailors, and tough times build greater people.* Coming out of
this intense season, I found that being tested through the
tempest storm produced a stronger, healthier, and wiser
person on the other side of it.

My marriage was strengthened in a new way. My wife,
Kelly, and I decided we would unite as our own family unit

to set a new course for the future of our family name. God showed me the importance of my calling now as the father of two beautiful young girls. I was given a deeper purpose for being a spiritual leader in my home after seeing the downfalls and ripple effects of what can happen in a family when poor decisions are continuously made.

Being told no for the dream job with the church led me to a much healthier and deeper spiritual place when it came to serving the church and how I view work. I developed more of an open-handed approach in life, knowing that whatever is given or taken away has a purpose behind it. I found that when you hold onto something in your hands so tightly that you won't let go, it causes two issues. First, you end up crushing the life out of what you have, squandering its potential. Second, you miss the opportunity to release what you are holding onto and create an open hand to receive something *better* that God has for you.

My encouragement to anyone going through a difficult trial is not to focus on what is happening to you but rather on who you can become. Learn to let go of what you can't control, and take ownership of what you can. Taking these actions will help you out of the victim mentality and put you back in the driver's seat of the areas you do have a say in. Even if you feel afraid, seek professional help. It benefitted me greatly and taught me that it's not what happens to you that matters the most; it's what *you decide to do with it.*

There is absolutely nothing that God cannot take hold of and ultimately turn it into good for our purpose and His glory. The greatest obstacles we face that seem, in the moment, overwhelmingly impossible, are finite and small from God's perspective. If you stop and reflect on this in the middle of the trial, you get an outside view of the issue you are facing and remind yourself of the bigger picture and purpose that God has for your life.

I found that one horrific year can be used to break generational sin and set a trajectory for living the life you only dreamed of, and the choice is yours!"

RESOURCES

The first step to stop abuse is to make the choice to get help. The following names of organizations and individuals are just a few of the many resources available to you, or someone you know, who is dealing with domestic violence.

The Internet is a vast source of information about abuse and people and places for support. Each state has help for domestic violence. By doing a search on *domestic violence help in (name of state)*, both the National Domestic Violence Hotline and resources near you will be listed. Your local police department is available to provide immediate help, answer questions, and refer you to local, state, and national organizations for assistance. Many counties have emergency and long-term shelters for battered women and their children, some in an undisclosed location for security.

National Domestic Violence Hotline
Website: https://www.thehotline.org
Phone: 1-800-799-SAFE (7233)

National Network to End Domestic Violence (NNEDV)

Website: https://nnedv.org/resources-library/national-network-end-domestic-violence/

Celebrate Recovery

Website: https://www.celebraterecovery.com

Dr. Erin Oksol, Psychologist

Email: drerinoksol@me.com

Website: www.drerinoksol.com

Sandra Russell, LMFT

Email: srussell@sandrarusselllmft.com

Phone: (916) 213-1017

SELF-CARE

Pamela Zimmer, Self-Care Concierge

"When I first heard the term "self-care," I was convinced it was a fancy way of saying, 'I get a massage once a month,' or 'I get my nails done.'

I have not been through abuse or trauma in the context of a marital relationship. However, the trauma of postpartum depression after my second son was born is still one that I find myself healing from. It took time, and eventually, I discovered that taking care of myself was the most kind and loving choice I could make for my family. What keeps me going and moving on a positive path, instead of spiraling back down into the darkness, is my self-care.

To the readers struggling to find the way after trauma and abuse, here is what I say to you. You are worth it! There is nothing more valuable than your health—mental, physical, and emotional—and it is your responsibility to nurture that. Find something that puts a smile on your face and brings an ease to your breath. Turn to God! Let Him speak truth and love and light into your life. Start small, even with just five minutes of focused breathing. Then, as you can, add more habits to your self-care practice. It won't happen overnight, but it will happen, and you are worth taking care of YOU!"

Wow, Pamela's words are powerful, especially for those of us who have experienced trauma and abuse. I encourage you to set aside some time in the next day or two, focus on what you've just read, and write down a few thoughts about your own self-care. Don't sabotage yourself with guilt from the past. You have an opportunity to change today and your future by starting with one simple self-care idea, practice it, and then add another. I suggest you keep the idea to yourself for a while or share it with someone you truly know has your best interest at heart. Unsafe people or your abuser will find this change of focus from them to you unsettling because it threatens their control over you.

Email: Pamela@PamelaZimmer.com

Website: www.pamelazimmer.com

Laura Bangar, Rodan + Fields

"I've been in the skincare industry for a decade now and recently expanded into haircare. I've had the honor of witnessing first-hand the impact a great skincare and haircare investment and routine can make on someone's life. Hearing Patty's story about her skin and how she is so happy with her results brings a smile to my face and immense joy.

After ten years, I not only love watching the impact great skincare and haircare have on women, but I appreciate it more than I ever have. It's always a wonderful feeling to help make someone feel good about themselves! I hope you give yourself permission to take care of yourself guilt free!

As a Christian, I believe the best glow comes from inside knowing <u>Who's</u> we are. I love helping people to know how loved and treasured they are by their Creator."

Email: <u>laurabangar@ymail.com</u>

Website: <u>www.laurabangar.com</u>

Thank you, Laura, for those words of encouragement to take care of ourselves, including our skin and hair. Here is my Rodan + Fields website if you would like more information: www.pattylauterjung.myrandf.com

Please take good care of yourself. You are valuable and worth it!

ABOUT THE AUTHOR

Patty Lauterjung is a Creative Solutions Strategist as a copy editor, writing coach, international bestselling author, and speaker. She has over twenty-five years of experience capturing the voice of others and turning their written words into bestselling books, dynamic websites, engaging marketing material, and online training programs. Her passion, priority, and purpose are to bring out the best in every client. Patty has a Bachelor of Arts in Business Management and is the owner of PL Creative Editing, LLC in Charlotte, NC.

Although most people find editing boring, Patty says, "I have one of the best jobs in the world!

My clients are fascinating, creative, and unique individuals. I bring my depth of knowledge, a broad range of editing experience, and commitment to exceed my clients' expectations to help them reach their audience in meaningful, engaging, and influential ways."

You can reach Patty at:

www.plcreativeediting.com
plcreativeediting@outlook.com
plenterprises7@gmail.com
www.facebook.com/PLCreativeEditing
www.linkedin.com/in/patty-lauterjung-a434699

Made in the USA
Columbia, SC
11 April 2023

14687369R00113